the

Shamanic Witch

the
Shamanic Witch

Spiritual Practice Rooted in the Earth and Other Realms

Gail Wood

FOREWORD BY KRISTIN MADDEN

WEISER BOOKS
San Francisco, CA / Newburyport, MA

First published in 2008 by
Red Wheel/Weiser, LLC
With offices at:
500 Third Street, Suite 230
San Francisco, CA 94107
www.redwheelweiser.com

ISBN: 978-1-57863-430-9

Library of Congress Cataloging-in-Publication Data is available upon request.

Cover and interior design by Maija Tollefson
Typeset in Minion
Cover photograph © Nick Free/iStockphoto

Printed in Canada
TCP
10 9 8 7 6 5 4 3 2 1

To my teacher, SunRaven, she that was
Your humor & wisdom continue to bless my path;
&
To Karel, she that is,
Devoted to the children of Epona,
Always an inspiration, teacher, and friend.
Thank you so much!
&
To LadyHawke, the Myth Maker,
Teacher, High Priestess, and dear friend.
Your vision and encouragement inspire me.
Thank you, dear sister.

CONTENTS

ACKNOWLEDGMENTS

No writer who produces a book that makes it into print works alone, even though writing can be a very solitary activity—although my dogs make sure I'm never truly alone anywhere in the house! There are a great many people and other beings that assisted and inspired this book. The interlibrary loan department of Memorial Library at SUNY Cortland, thank you for your tireless and first-class efforts to get information into the hands of those who need it!

My teacher, SunRaven, continues to inspire me to dance and sing with the drum. To my High Priestess, LadyHawk, who issued the challenge to write on shamanic journeywork for our tradition, this book is the result. To the Foundation of Light in Ithaca, New York, for providing the place for drumming and journeywork, and to Sharon for passing the torch onto Mouse and me—thank you very much! And to the group itself and all the devoted and occasional members for your inspiring work.

To the RavenMyst Circle, my witchy brothers and sisters, thank you so much for your inspiration, support, and encouragement. Most especially to the Coven of the Heron and to the Coven of the Redtail Hawk—you are all as magical as our totems.

To my scribbling brothers and sisters of Witches in Print, thank you for sharing your struggles, your joys, and your triumphs. I have learned a lot about the life of a writer and the life of an author from all of you. And to our list-witch, Maggie Shayne, your generosity and humanness is inspiring.

To the kind and wonderful folks at Red Wheel/Weiser, thank you for your support and assistance. To Brenda Knight, who started the process, and Amber Guetebier, who has nursed this book along. Thanks to everyone.

To Mouse, all my love and all my thanks.

FOREWORD

Raised in a shamanic home by the family deathwalker, I grew up in an environment where trance states were a normal daily experience. The spirits of the dead, "totem" animals, and spirits of place were common visitors and residents with us. I was trained from a very young age to develop the ability we all share to travel out of body and interact with other worlds.

As a young teenager, I became interested in Witchcraft. It seemed like simply another branch of the tradition that my family already lived. I embraced new ways of ritual, magick, and connecting with the Divine. In fact, I defined myself as a witch for fifteen years. It was only when I began interacting more and more with Neopagans that I saw the differences in the paths and realized that, although very similar, I didn't quite fit in with the wiccan witches I was encountering. And yet the "family resemblance" was so intriguing that I decided it must be a case of divergent evolution.

Then, nearly ten years ago, I had some interesting conversations with noted teachers Janet Farrar and Gavin Bone about the possible shamanic roots of Witchcraft. I even drummed for one of Gavin's classes at a festival around that time, which was the beginning of a new chapter in the communal perception of these practices. Since then, I have seen a great many witches seeking a shamanic complement to their spiritual journeys. My classes at Ardantane and around the country regularly fill up with witches seeking new ways to connect with Deity and their own ecstatic roots. In the last few years, the term "Shamanic Witchcraft" has gained popularity, offering a new, or perhaps ancient, twist on this spiritual practice.

The term "ecstasy" comes from a Greek root meaning "to stand outside." It is a subjective experience of transcendence, during which the individual achieves a heightened sense of awareness, altered states of consciousness, and seems to be outside normal time and space. Long attributed to shamans, the ecstatic trance is part of our ancient spiritual heritage. And it is something shared by a great many witches.

Many people have difficulty defining just what it is that separated Witchcraft and Shamanism in modern times. Gail Wood helps us to appreciate each path as simply sides to the same spiritual coin. In general, witches tend to call in the energies they need, bringing the other worlds to them and working external, often more structured, magic. Shamans (or shamanic practitioners) tend to work predominantly in trance states, traveling to the other worlds, and working a more subtle magic with the intent to heal or delve into one's personal shadows. A perception has grown around this, labeling shamans as "darker" and more solitary practitioners, while witches have gotten a bad rap as being outwardly focused and not as serious in their spirituality. Neither is an accurate description, so I am glad to see books like this dispelling these myths and offering a new look at these empowering paths of honor and ecstasy.

In 2006, I had the great pleasure of being a part of one of Gail's Shamanic Witchcraft circles. It was one of the most powerful rituals I have ever been blessed to participate in, and my son still maintains that it was the best public ritual he has ever attended. Gail merges shamanic elements into a Craft framework, drawing equally on both practices to create a truly transformative experience. I have been honored to share in conversations with her, both online and in person, and she is someone for whom I have great respect. She brings her inspired intelligence and creativity to her writing, providing a book that is provocative, down-to-earth, and accessible for anyone.

This is a book that should be on the bookshelf of anyone interested in mystic paths, particularly alternative or pagan paths. Gail deftly weaves a guide that really does allow the reader to "shift shape and move through time, space, and thought." Following the concepts and practices laid out in this book offers something beyond basic core Shamanism and Witchcraft—it reminds you of your own innate shamanic abilities and teaches you to put those abilities into practice as a shamanic witch. Gail has created a powerful practice that can show you the way to walk between the worlds with great personal power and deep insight, not only into the energetic and magical workings of the multiverse, but also of your own self.

—Kristin Madden, author of *The Shamanic Guide to Death and Dying* and *The Book of Shamanic Healing*

In All the Empty Places

May the Spirits be with you
In all the empty places
In all the empty places that you walk.
Guardian of your heart,
Companion to your soul,
May the Spirits be with you
In all the empty places that you walk.

May the Spirits be with you
In all the crowded places
In all the crowded places that you walk.
Protector of your body,
Healer of your love,
May the Spirits be with you
In all the crowded places that you walk.

May the Spirits be with you
In all the sacred places
In all the sacred places that you walk.
Loving the Goddess,
Embracing the God,
May the Spirits be with you
In all the sacred places that you walk.

CHAPTER 1

The Dance of Ecstasy: First Steps on the Path of Shamanic Wicca

We are the flow and we are the ebb,
We are the needle and we are the thread.
We are the spider and we are the web,
We are the witches, back from the dead!

As witches we move in magic, spiraling in and out of the energies of this world and other worlds. We shift shape and move through time, space, and thought. Our connections to the world of Spirit assist us in moving into the magic. The opening chant tells us that

we are part of everything, and nothing holds us back. Another chant
tells us of our place and role in this universal flow of energy:

> Spiraling into the center, the center of the wheel
> We are the weavers, we are the woven ones
> We are the dreamers, we are the dream.

The thread of divine within us weaves with the thread of the divine throughout all the worlds, creating patterns of beauty, joy, and transformation. We are both active and passive in the flow of universal energy; we are both the product and the producer. We are everything as we embrace all the energies of the worlds, weaving a tapestry of mystery and power.

In embracing Shamanism as part of the path of Wicca, we are doing something incredibly ancient and something thoroughly modern. The roots of modern Shamanism are found in every culture, living and dead. The abilities of the shaman are the abilities of the modern witch, reaching back thousands of years into the fire-lit caves of the first humans. As we walk and dance our paths, we circle inward to learn what came before, and then we spiral outward to create new ways of magic for ourselves, those we love, and the Universe as a whole.

This book takes the basic instructions in the modern practice of core Shamanism and melds them with the magical practices of Wicca and Witchcraft. While the magical practices are wiccan in focus, they have broad application for anyone seeking alternatives to mainstream religions. It is also a guide for someone who follows a pagan practice and also does shamanic journey-work. It has been my observation that most pagans and wiccans practicing shamanic journeywork keep those practices separate. This book provides a guide for melding those two practices into a dynamic dance of ecstasy and joy.

I took my first introduction to shamanic drumming class around the same time I began my exploration of Wicca and Tarot. Throughout more than twenty years of exploration, I have melded these three practices together, along with other skills and knowledge that I picked up along the way. Our lives and how we live them are interconnected, all together weaving a beautiful picture. It takes a long time, sometimes, to see how all the individual threads intertwine, interweave, and interconnect. The beauty of it is that all of us are doing this same kind of weaving, and then, as we move together, we overlap and intertwine our own patterns within this greater whole. If we are lucky, we glimpse the beautiful whole. Throughout it all, our inner divine nature dances with the Divine Universe that we call Goddess and God. Their steps and ours interweave in beauty and love.

Shamanic practice seeks healing and wisdom from realms that overlap ours. The practitioner journeys into those realms to find answers, healing, power, and mastery for the individual practitioner and for community. Wicca casts a circle and calls in the wise ones from realms that overlap ours. In that circle between the worlds, the witch journeys and communes with the creatures and teachers of those realms for the same reasons—to find power, answers, healing, and mastery. Both the shamanic practitioner and the witch bring that wisdom back to help and heal themselves and others. In an alchemical melding, the shamanic practitioner and the witch become one in service to self, to others and to the Goddess and God.

In the past several years, I have deliberately and consciously melded my solitary wiccan practice with my shamanic skills. My experiences have taught me about the profound nature of these two practices and how to create connections between them. In many ways, the connections are natural because both practices have much in common. It is a dance, a walk between the worlds and back again. This book is a guide to combining the two worlds of Shamanism and Witchcraft.

The Journey of Shamanism into Popular Culture and Spiritual Life

Most of the scholarly work on Shamanism was done by historians and anthropologists, and the study of Shamanism in popular culture has a definite anthropological and scholarly twist. There are extensive scholarly studies of shamans, shamanic healing, and the use of trance in native cultures. This has been problematic for the indigenous cultures being studied because early anthropologists often interpreted their observations through the lens of their own cultural assumptions, calling indigenous shamans madmen and charlatans. The observations made by early anthropologists were often judgmental and in error. Even with these problems, the study of Shamanism by anthropologists and social scientists has brought a large body of knowledge to the public. Historian and religious scholar Mircea Eliade's studies such as *Shamanism: Archaic Techniques of Ecstasy* remain the foundational work on understanding the role of the shaman in society and religion. It was Eliade who first described shamans as "technicians of ecstasy."

Shamans used singing, dancing, and drumming to achieve their ecstatic states, but it was the use of plant medicines to enhance their awareness that brought Shamanism to the attention of popular culture. Situated in their own culture, the use of perception-altering drugs by these native shamans was appropriate and purposeful. Unfortunately, what evolved was an understanding by outsiders that drugs were needed to achieve these states of wisdom, or that the shamanic trance work was pursued in order to experience drug-induced states of euphoria. Awareness of shamanic trance work, along with its relationship to hallucinogenic drugs, made its way into the popular consciousness with the publication of a 1957 article in *Life* magazine, entitled "Seeking the Magic Mushroom" by R. Gordon Wasson, triggered an interest in shamanic trance techniques by the general public.[1] That interest was further piqued by the publication of a series of books, beginning in 1968, by an academic anthropologist named Carlos Casteneda who chronicled his studies with a Yaqui Indian sorcerer named Don Juan. Even though anthropologists and others questioned the veracity of Casteneda's works, the books captured the popular imagination and interest.

In 1980, anthropologist Michael Harner further popularized Shamanism with the publication of *The Way of the Shaman*, which describes his work with the Jivaro and Coniba Indians and described methods that readers could use to achieve the altered states he described without drugs. Harner went on to establish The Foundation for Shamanic Studies, which teaches these techniques worldwide. He and his teachers use the term "core Shamanism" to describe the set of skills and techniques that anyone in any culture can use to explore trance states.

At about the same time, psychologists became interested in the shamanic trance states, seeing these altered states of consciousness as a way to study human behavior. Psychologists began using trance states along with hypnosis to assist people in overcoming a myriad of emotional problems, history, and challenges. This dovetailed with the New Age movement's interest in self-improvement and self-actualization, and the movement used hypnosis and altered states for self-improvement and spiritual awakenings.

Shamanism and shamanic techniques have made their mark on the pagan community as well, particularly in the United States. In the 1995 study of American paganism, *Never Again the Burning Times: Paganism Revived*, author and pagan practitioner Loretta Orion states that American Wicca has evolved from its British Witchcraft roots through the influence of four factors: (1) ritual style developed from large outdoor gatherings; (2) the presence of workshops on shamanic techniques; (3) the concept of the earth as a living, conscious, Divine being; and, (4) the presence of a psychotherapy model and its application to political activism.[2] In addition, the integration of these ritual and shamanic techniques into personal and group practice has had a large influence on American Wicca.

This idea is echoed by Karen E. Goeller in scholar Chas Clifton's 1994 collection of essays in *Witchcraft Today, Book Three: Witchcraft & Shamanism*. Goeller writes of the differences between the Craft and Shamanism, saying:

> Another essential difference between the Craft and Shamanism, at least in modern times, deals with the nature of the spiritual experience. Craft rituals are true celebratory rites, ripe with laughter, joy, positive feelings, and positive energy. Most work done by witches in recent years, ritually speaking, has been on

the positive side in an attempt to balance the perceived negatives pouring in from the rest of society. Shamanism takes a somewhat narrower and darker view. Much of Shamanism deals with death and the experience thus takes on a heavier, darker tone. The work being attempted is serious and often frightening . . ."[3]

In another essay, editor Chas Clifton writes that a witch commented to him that "[i]t seems that shamans do much more of their work on the other planes, while the Craft works more on this plane. We tend to call our Guardians, Watchers, and Deities to our circle, rather than to wander out to meet them."[4] Clifton agrees with this statement by saying that witches do often celebrate and create magick without the use of the ecstatic trance state, instead using a state of heightened awareness.

In the decade or so since the collection of essays was published, both Wicca and Shamanism have merged closer together in balance and focus. For many practitioners of the Craft, Wicca is not a happy-go-lucky spiritual path that celebrates only things associated with the lighter side of spirituality. Throughout the pagan world, Wicca has gained an underserved reputation for being shallow, or what pagan communities often term "fluffy-bunny," when, in actuality, the spiritual path of Wicca has stepped boldly forward to face death, mental illness, and disease, as well as the joyful celebration of life. Wiccans recognize that life is not "Tra-la-la, we all love the Goddess," and is a religion that travels through the realms of magic in service of the Gods and one another. This is precisely what Shamanism does as well. When a witch calls the guardians and spirits into the circle, a partnership develops where the spirits work with the witch to create sacred space, an act very similar to a shaman working with spirit allies to heal or find information. In the last decade, the practices of Witchcraft and the practices of Shamanism have moved closer together, with each augmenting and enhancing the other. Witchcraft brings, in part, the belief and the religion, while Shamanism brings the skill and the practice.

Definitions of Modern Shamanism

Throughout the world and throughout time, societies have had members of their social structures who are healers, medicine men, and spiritual leaders. These healers, who are either men or women, enter a trance state, where, assisted by spirit guides, they travel other realities in search of answers to questions, for healing, for power, and for understanding. Michael Harner wrote in *The Way of the Shaman*, that the "shaman is a man or a woman who enters an altered state of consciousness at will to contact and utilize an ordinary hidden reality in order to acquire knowledge, power, and to help other persons. The shaman has at least one and usually more spirit assistants and guides at his personal service."[5] Shamans were different from other spiritual and healing practitioners because they had otherworldly assistance, moved out of themselves to travel to other worlds, and because they performed these tasks in the service of others, family, friends, and community.

The term "shaman" is derived from the language of the Tungus people of Siberia; their "saman" means one who is excited, moved, and raised. Roger Walsh writes in *The Spirit of Shamanism* that the term "shaman" has been "widely adopted to refer to specific groups of healers in diverse cultures who have sometimes been called medicine men, witch doctors, sorcerers, wizards, magicians or seers."

Walsh goes on to define Shamanism as "a family of traditions whose practitioners focus on voluntarily entering altered states of consciousness in which they experience themselves or their spirit(s), traveling to other realms at will, and interacting with other entities in order to serve their communities."[6] Another expression used to describe a shaman is "the one who walks between the worlds," signifying the shaman's ability to travel out of body into other dimensions.

The definitions of Shamanism focus on the method, not the beliefs. Shamanism is not seen as a religion, but as a social, religious, and spiritual tradition. Although the techniques are not considered a religion, shamans integrate these skills with their own religious beliefs. What distinguishes shamans from other religious and spiritual mediators is the shaman's interaction with spirits, especially their ability to control their own states of consciousness. Most frequently these altered states are referred to as "ecstatic states," in that the shaman employs techniques of ecstasy. To those of us living in the modern world, the state of ecstasy is most often aligned with sexual intercourse and sexual feeling. Indeed, sexual pleasure is one example of ecstasy and ecstatic state. A good working definition of ecstasy for the modern practitioner is the concept of moving out of one's normal state of consciousness and entering into a state of heightened feeling. These states of ecstasy can include experiences of soul flight, where the state is experienced as the soul leaving the body. They can also include traveling into a hidden aspect of reality.

Michael Harner explains that "in Shamanism, the maintenance of one's personal power is fundamental to well-being."[7] It awakens what is already present in the person and the work of the shaman is to maintain a high level of powerful functioning. What distinguishes this aspect of Shamanism from sorcery is that the shaman works on personal power as service to others, while a sorcerer works to gain power solely for self and for gain. The shamanic life is one of training and discipline, where training comes both from the inner and outer worlds. The authentic shamanic experience is the authentic personal experience. There are no standard experiences, maps, or guides. As the shaman journeys and learns, the shaman grows in power and understanding.

As witches, we have an advantage when learning Shamanism. The training in meditation and the movement of energy in ritual and spell work give the witch knowledge of how the energy of the Universe works. The witch already sees herself as the tool through which energy flows and is directed. In addition, the witch usually has an understanding of one or more divination techniques and is accustomed to the idea that wisdom comes from a variety of places both within and outside of the self. The witch knows that insight comes from within, from the symbolism present in the natural world, and from other worlds.

CHAPTER 2

The Realms of the Shamanic Practitioner: Understanding the World of the Shaman

To the drumbeat, we enter the realm of the shamanic practitioner. Firelight dances and casts shadows on the walls of our hearts as we reach deep within ourselves to move outward into the realms of spirit and mystery. At first the worlds are unfamiliar, but with practice we are able to move into the flow of power and energy and the worlds of the shaman become familiar territory. As we grow in strength and wisdom, we seek to go further and deeper into the mystery.

The Shamanic Cosmos

The witch's idea that all time and place is fluid fits with the concept of the shaman walking across the worlds, accessing inner landscapes and other worlds to find wisdom. Both the shaman and the witch understand that all life is connected and what one creature does affect all others. Moreover, the worlds that meld together are the worlds of the physical and the spiritual. In Shamanism, there is an understanding that there is an ordinary reality and a nonordinary reality, to use terms coined by Carlos Castaneda. Then nonordinary reality is the world that is hidden and cannot be viewed or sensed by our physical senses. This reality is known by different names by different cultures; the Void, the parallel universe, the Otherworld, and the Dreamtime are all names for the cosmos that intersects with our earth world, or ordinary reality. None of these realities is better than the other; these are terms to distinguish how the realities are perceived, sensed, and understood.

There are levels of nonordinary reality, just as there are levels within our own ordinary reality. The cosmos of the shaman is divided into three: the Upper World, Lower World, and Middle World. These are not hierarchical levels, but rather terms of reference based on our experiences and understanding of shamanic journeywork. Typically the experiences of shamans fall into these categories, but often individual experiences will vary; while there are three levels in this concept of the cosmos, it is really a multidimensional Universe with many facets and many different landscapes. The shaman journeys to and around each of these worlds.

The Upper World is the place of spirit guides, teachers, and the Wise Ones, i.e., beings that people may consider Gods, Goddesses,

Angels, or other beings Divine or special beings within an individual's belief system. It is the place of learning on all levels using the mind, the heart, and the soul. This world is not usually considered Heaven in the sense that practitioners of mainstream religions conceive of it as a reward for earthly good behavior. The Upper World is not directly above our heads in the cosmos, but above our heads in the other realms that intersect with our reality.

The Lower World is the place of animal helpers, guardian spirits, and power animals. It is the place of instinctual learning, imaginative feeling, and broad thinking. Even though it is also called the Underworld, it is not conceived as a place of eternal damnation or exclusively the land of the dead. The Lower World is located beneath our feet in those parallel places that overlap our reality.

The Middle World is this world, our reality, and even though it is referred to as ordinary reality, there are many mysteries and hidden treasures to be explored through shamanic journeywork. Within the Middle World, some traditions believe there are other Kingdoms, such as the Animal Kingdom, the Human Kingdom, the Plant Kingdom, and the Mineral Kingdom. Also inhabiting this world are the Elementals, and other spirits that serve as helpers or guardians to the creatures, plants, and minerals inhabiting the Middle World. The intersecting worlds in the Middle World create a multidimensional interweaving of life.

The Axis Mundi, often called the World Tree, is the energy that links these three worlds together. The roots of the Tree extend deep into the Lower World and the branches reach far into the Upper World. The Tree puts out leaves and bears fruit in the Middle World. The sap, the lifeblood of the Tree, flows between all the worlds, connecting and bringing unity to them. I believe the energy that links these worlds together is maintained and made stronger by the walkers between the worlds, the witch and the shaman. The partnership developed through shamanic work and magical work creates living, sacred connections between the worlds.

The reality and landscape of these worlds is in the experiences of the shaman who journeys through them. Nothing is right or wrong—it is all within the power and understanding of the person who journeys through them. While written authorities make statements about which spirits inhabit the different levels of reality, it is important to realize that the most authentic authority is the practitioner, the one who walks between the worlds.

When we, as witches, meld our magical practices with shamanic journeywork, we boldly become the Witch-Shaman, or Shamanic Witch. The direct, ecstatic experience of the Divine through the God and Goddess brings us the same kind of wisdom, power, and understanding that the ancient peoples had of their world. When we do our magic and our journeywork in service of our Craft, our family, and our community, we transform the self-improvement movement back into an experience of the mysteries of the Universe.

Living in these worlds are spirit allies that work with us, teach us, and join with us as we do our magical and healing work. These spirits and creatures come to us in animal form and human form, and can be found in all the worlds, Upper, Middle, and Lower. Our guardian spirits come to us in the form of animals and usually inhabit the Lower World. These animal spirits work with us in a variety of roles, sometimes for a lifetime and sometimes as we work on and work out particular issues in our lives. Called "power animals," these creatures accompany us on our life journeys, assisting us in our discoveries and adventures. Animals of the natural world, of areas of the world unfamiliar to us, extinct creatures, and mythological animals can all be animal allies for us in our work.

The teachers who guide us and give us wisdom appear most often in the Upper World, and can be in human or near-human form. Angels, deities, heroes, and admired public figures can all manifest as our teachers.

Other creatures can also show themselves as helping guides, appearing in the Middle World, Upper World, and Lower World. The devas and resident spirits of animals and plants can show themselves to us. Faeries and other creatures of worlds hidden from our ordinary consciousness can be a part of this journey. The guardians of the directions and elemental spirits of all kinds may show themselves and be willing to work with you.

When working with the creatures and spirits of these Worlds, it is important to be thankful, polite, and grateful for their assistance. They are our allies and it is important to maintain relationships with them, by wearing their image, researching them as they manifest in the natural world, and working with them to understand their spiritual nature as well as their natural one. This strengthens our relationship with them. It keeps our own energy vibrant and strong as we maintain our vital link with them. The ancient peoples believed that one of the reasons a person weakened, sickened, and grew listless was that their relationship with their spirit allies had become broken or was not maintained in an honorable way.

As the Shamanic Witch journeys regularly and builds relationships with the helping spirit allies, the understanding of the cosmos deepens, taking on richness, texture, and sophisticated understanding that includes both breadth and depth. As the Witch-Shaman works with this melding of magic and ecstasy in ritual and in magick, the allies of all the worlds enter into the circle as partners, friends, and co-creators of the mysteries. The Shamanic Witch moves with the energies as they dance within her and through her to create new worlds in service to self, the community, and the Gods.

States of Consciousness and the Experience of Shamanic Journeywork

In discussions of the trance work of Shamanism, two terms coined by Michael Harner are used: Ordinary State of Consciousness (OSC) and Shamanic State of Consciousness (SSC). OSC is the consciousness of our everyday waking selves and SSC is the ecstatic trance state used when shamans travel between the worlds. The SSC allows the practitioner to remember the experience when returning to ordinary states of awareness. According to most writers on shamanic practice, the SSC is achieved through drumming, chanting, and singing. Witches attain this state of consciousness through these methods, and also through meditation, visualization, and astral projection.

Hypnotherapy also provides some understanding of these states. The trance states are as follows:

- **Beta:** Our awake and conscious mind; engages in linear functions. Concentration and ability to complete a task are hallmarks of this state.

- **Alpha:** A light trance, a state of heightened awareness of all senses. Daydreaming, reading, meditation, grounding, and centering are all examples of the alpha state.

- **Theta:** A deep trance, a state of heightened creativity. Meditation, guided meditation, and astral projection are all examples of what can be done in this state.

- **Delta:** A profound sleep and somnambulist state. This is where state hypnotists place their subjects because people are highly suggestible.

The SSC is the theta state of consciousness. The shaman maintains a high state of awareness and all the senses are aware in this state, but the outer world recedes into the background. Ideally, all anxiety falls away and the journey begins to deepen. It is the ability to move between the worlds and, with the help of spirit allies, find information and help that distinguishes the shamanic practice from other types of magical and healing practices. Through drum, dance, and song, the shaman finds hope and joy while traveling through the cosmos.

The use of the term "trance" has a specific meaning in this context. Trance is not a blank state empty of consciousness and intelligence where the practitioner is powerless to control the vision. Rather, trance is an active state of consciousness where the shamanic practitioner is aware, lucid, and in control. Our ability to understand the magical worlds the shaman is about to enter becomes heightened. In trance, through power and will, the shamanic practitioner is in control of the trance and how the journey unfolds. The practitioner is able to break the trance if necessary, or to continue on as necessary. The journey does not happen *to* the practitioner, but this walker between the worlds is an active participant, asking questions and seeking wisdom.

When confronted with the word "trance," many people become intimidated, thinking that trance is some esoteric skill that comes with discipline. The kind of intentional trance of the shaman is something that takes practice to develop, but every human being trances. Trance is a kind of hypnosis, another word that can intimidate people. But everyone does it. You know those long drives on monotonous roads when suddenly you realize you don't know where the last forty miles have gone? Or when you concentrate on a really good book, project, or activity and become lost in it? Those situations are examples of trance. When you watch television and lose your awareness of what's going on around you, that is not only trance, but self-hypnosis as well. Everyone has this skill, which is necessary in order to be able to do the things they need to do and love to do. To enter into the Shamanic State of Consciousness, you just harness your innate abilities and direct them to your stated purposes.

The spirits and creatures of the other realms speak to us in symbols. In many cases, their messages seem like riddles and in other cases, these symbols feel so familiar we fear we are just imagining their presence. Spirits use symbols familiar to us so that we can achieve a better understanding of their messages. These can include cartoon characters and other popular culture images, childhood memories, and anything that causes a sense of recognition and resonance. You can trust your gut because Spirit is working with your imagination and memory to send you wisdom.

A common concern from beginning and experienced practitioners is often expressed as, "I'm not sure I'm doing this right." In our media-saturated environment, we often have unrealistic expectations about what our meditative visions will look like. We may fall into the expectation that the journeys will look like a television program or a movie with wonderful visual effects and a coherent, logical narrative. That is not usually the case, and if we give up the expectation of doing it right, we will be blessed with insight and wisdom. Most people experience meditations in one of three ways, or they will have experiences that overlap these extrasensory ways of seeing. Some people, known as clairvoyants, will see the journeys and experiences them with as visions and visuals. Other people, called clairaudients, will hear their journeys and experiences them as messages, voices, or even a narration. Still others, the clairsentients, will feel their journeys, experiencing the meditations kinesthetically with their bodies; they will feel the journey physically, even sometimes including smells. I tend not to be visual, but a combination of audient and sentient. I have found it useful to ask questions such as, "Who is here?" or "What is happening now?" Answers to my questions will usually manifest themselves. Below, you will find a guided meditation that will help you determine which kind of meditation is the strongest. Remember, you will experience all three types of meditation as you practice trance and meditation, though one will continue to be the strongest.

Sometimes our preconceived ideas about ourselves may prevent us from understanding the messages delivered to us during journeying. If we think we are visual learners and we do not see in a journey, we may think we are doing something wrong. Our conscious minds understand the world in a particular way and that influences how we learn. How we are and how we learn in ordinary reality may not be the way we learn and perceive in nonordinary reality. In nonordinary reality, other parts of our mind and soul are at work. I am a very visually oriented learner in ordinary reality, and, as I have said before, I am strongly clairsentient in nonordinary reality. The world of Spirit is providing me with opportunities to understand things in a different way. Quite literally, I am getting out of my head and into my body when I walk between the worlds. We have to let go of our expectations and let the world of Spirit speak to us in a myriad of ways. Remember, too, that you are not all one thing, but a wonderful combination of all things. If you are stronger in one area, you can work with that strength. If you are weaker in another area, you can make that weakness stronger and more effective.

The experiences within a journey will also vary in marvelous ways. Some people are right there in the middle of the action, singing, dancing, cooking, building and having all the experiences. Others will be active onlookers, following the action but not necessarily an integral part. Often all kinds of interaction will occur within a journey. Whatever happens, you *are* the active participant in your journey. I have had the experience where there is a narrator, either myself or another, and I have had to discern whether I was second-guessing everything, or whether I was receiving help from my spirit allies. Discernment and understanding are very helpful skills to have when journeying into the realms of Spirit.

Seeing, Hearing, and Feeling: A Guided Visualization for Understanding How You Perceive in Meditations and Journeying

Inhale deeply and fully, drawing breath from every part of your being, and hold it for a couple of seconds. On the exhale, breathe out expectations. Inhale deeply again, drawing in magic; hold your breath for a couple of seconds. On the exhale, breathe out worries and care. Inhale deeply, drawing in serenity; hold your breath for a couple of seconds. On the exhale, breathe out a tone (ommmmm). Continue to breathe deeply as you close your eyes.

You find yourself in your favorite place in the whole world. Look around and drink in the beauty of this wonderful place. Breathe in all the things that make this your favorite place. Notice all the ideas, feelings, and aspects that make this a place of happiness. Look around and breathe in this wonderful place.

(pause)

There before you, you see something glimmering in the light. You kneel down and pick it up. It is a golden coin and you know that it will bring you millions.

(pause)

Put the object in your pocket. Notice before you that there is a table with a bowl of fruit. Sit down, and pick an orange from the bowl; peel it, and eat a juicy section.

(pause)

When you are finished eating, take a deep breath, and suddenly you see the Goddess sitting at the table across from you. She speaks to you about the wisdom and power of this place.

(pause)

When she is finished, she gives you a small gift, something to symbolize your life as a walker between the worlds, and you tell her thank you. And with that, she is gone in a twinkling of an eye.

With a deep breath, you are back in your sacred space. With a second breath, you are fully in your body, and with a long deep breath, you open your eyes.

The second part of this exercise is to write about it. As you are writing, answer the following questions.

- How did you feel when you found the golden object worth a million dollars? Where did you feel the emotions—in your head, heart, or in your body?

- How did you experience peeling and eating the orange? Did you see the peel? Did you smell the orange and feel the juice on your hands and fingers? Did you taste the orange as you ate it?

- When the Goddess spoke to you, did you hear her words or did you just know what she said? Did you feel her put the object in her hands, or did you see her put it there?

People who are clairvoyant see things more often than they feel the other sensations. In this meditation, a clairvoyant person might see their favorite place and note in detail what is in their surroundings. They would see the glimmer of gold of the million-dollar object. They would see the orange very clearly while the tastes and smell might not be something they experience.

Clairaudient people might hear something like a voice narrating the experience. In this case, you have to be careful that you are hearing the meditations and not your own inner self-criticizing voice. It is easy to distinguish; the inner critic is talking in dos and don'ts, while the clairaudient perception is more neutral and observing. Hearing the voice of the Goddess rather than noticing what she looks like is a clairaudient talent.

Clairsentient people will experience a meditation as sensations and feeling. They might smell the orange and feel the stinging of the juice, but they might not see a thing. The wisdom of the Goddess is revealed as "knowing" rather than hearing or seeing anything. You might know that your gift is a feather or other object, but never see it.

As I have said before, we are a combination of these meditation skills, with one stronger than the others. We can also develop our skills over time and with practice. It takes time to develop strong journeying and meditation skills. It also takes a lot of self-love and forgiveness to know that whatever way you do it or feel it is the right way. In groups, it can be very easy to judge yourself as lacking when someone else is a vivid clairvoyant and describes their journeys well. Know that you are just as good as they are; your skill may be different. The wonderful pictures are not yours, but you still feel or hear the messages of the Divine. That is the important thing. Keep your heart open and your soul eager to learn, and the world of Spirit will welcome you and bless your path as you walk between the worlds.

Becoming a Shamanic Practitioner

As you embark on this work, it is important to realize that there is sensitivity among indigenous peoples throughout the world that people of the industrialized countries sometimes do not recognize. The native peoples feel that the dominant culture has purchased or stolen not only their lands and language, but also their spirituality. Ranging from rage and anger to concern, these feelings are expressed in a variety of ways and forums. In order to honor the legacy from indigenous peoples, an ethic has developed to not call oneself a shaman, a term most often reserved for people raised in traditional cultures. Rather, modern practitioners call this practice

Neoshamanism, and call practitioners a variety of terms including shamanic practitioners. If you join Neoshamanic groups in person or online, calling oneself a shaman is one of the first things that gets corrected; otherwise, it creates a barrier between the individual and the group.

Another reason to not claim the title of shaman is that the role of a shaman, particularly in indigenous cultures, is one that is not taken, but is given after a series of trials and tests. In addition, like many initiatory practices, there is a feeling that the title and initiation is given by Spirit and not taken by the person. Often when a title such as shaman is taken by an individual, the person is prone to arrogance or pride—two qualities that drain away sincerity and compassion, leaving only an empty title.

Shamanism and shamanic techniques are practiced throughout the world and throughout time, and the ability to use these techniques is resident within each individual. It is not theft to begin practicing them, but a reemergence of skills and abilities. It is good to be aware of the anger and concern, so that you do not accidentally, with the best intentions in the world, offend someone. Taking care with your language and your practices shows a respect and awareness that is appropriate to the witches who seek to do no harm. It is a fine line, too, because often the world of Spirit calls out to us in forms that we understand and that can include symbols and attributes affiliated and associated with native peoples.

I believe that it is an act of daring and transformative power to claim the name of Witch-Shaman. It is an assertion of our ability to meld many skills together in the service of our Gods, our planet, and ourselves. Just as Shamanism seeks the direct experience of ecstasy, so too does the witch. Melding these two names together creates an alchemical energy of grace, beauty, and power. This is done in service, carrying on the intentions of Shamanism practiced throughout the world. For the good of all and the harm of none, the Shamanic Witch journeys to other realms for wisdom, healing, and transformation.

The Shamanic Journey

The drumbeat calls to us to move to other realms. The beating of the drum echoes the rhythm of the earth and the Universe. It pulls us through our own rhythms, the beating of our hearts, and the pounding of our blood. We heed the call and tune ourselves to the rhythms of that drum. That attunement is called entrainment, or entraining, which is the power of one rhythm to move into harmony with another. Naturally seeking resonance, we see entrainment all the time. When we spontaneously clap, sing, or hum along with a song we hear, or when our footsteps move to the beat of a song, or when we dance. Shamanic journeywork begins with moving into resonance with the heartbeat of the drum.

Typically, the modern shaman journeys to the other realms via the beat of a drum (or the recorded drumbeat). The terms "journey" and "journeywork" are used to describe this basic function. The drum is beat at 205-220 beats per minute so that SSC can be achieved. It is often hard for even an experienced journeyer to drum and journey at the same time, so having assistance either with a drummer or by electronic means is often helpful for the beginning journeyer. Once the journey is completed, the drummer signals the return by changing the pace of the drumming, usually four loud, slow beats followed by an accelerated tempo.

For the modern practitioner, most journeywork is done in a physically comfortable environment, in darkness or semidarkness. Using an eye mask or scarf to cover the eyes is appropriate. I often journey with my arm over my eyes. Often in trance, the body temperature will drop, so wearing socks or having a light blanket as covering is a good idea. As you begin to journey, get comfortable; whether you prefer to sit or lie down is a matter of personal preference.

To have an effective journey, it is important to focus on a question or statement. State your intention and where you want to go to get the answers. You should be able to state your intention clearly and simply, even for the most complex questions. Multiple goals or intentions can often result in mixed messages from the world of Spirit. I was taught an extremely effective way to do this: take three centering breaths and continue to breathe deeply, and state the intention three times. For instance, "I am going to the Upper World to ask my teachers about whether to go on for my Ph.D.," is a good example of a well-stated journey.

Attitude is important in journeywork. It is always good to let go of preconceived notions that may limit the world of Spirit, or that may blind you to the messages that are intended for you. Openness and hopefulness are good ways to approach journeywork. Understand where you many have expectations, good and bad. Remember that this is often deep inner work, and be aware that you might get messages or information that makes you uncomfortable or unhappy. Work through the messages and your feelings to find the inner wisdom that they contain. Spirit works with and through you to help you, so what you bring to the situation is very valid.

The shamanic journey is an adventure and a passage to a place of great wisdom. To be a shamanic practitioner, you must practice.

Journey often and listen to the wisdom of the work. Integrate the wisdom you have gained into your everyday life. It is an excellent practice to record your journeys. You will be surprised how much you forget, and often the wisdom of the journeys will not manifest for a long time. Keeping a record, whether it is in writing or by other means, is an important part of your practice. Many shamanic practitioners find that they open up to creativity in ways that they have never experienced before, so in addition to developing a practice of recording your journeys, also develop new ways of expression through art, dance, writing, gardening, or whatever calls to your heart and your spirit.

Preparing for Your Journey

Preparation is important in shamanic journeywork. Often, we find the distractions of our lives and our environment a large inhibiting factor in successful trance work. It is not that hard to avoid these distractions with a little good preparation. Journeys are more satisfying and helpful if we plan and prepare ourselves for the adventure ahead.

Prepare the Space

Find a space where you can comfortably go into trance without interruption. Turn off the phone and other distracting mechanical devices, including things that might be operating under your daily awareness. I can't tell you how distracting a ticking clock can become when everything becomes quiet and you are attempting to go into trance. You didn't notice it before, but now it is all you can hear!

Prepare the space in a way that makes the place a passage away from the distractions of your daily life and a portal into the realms of magic. Clean the space both physically and energetically. You can dispel any lingering energetic distractions by rattling the space with a rattle. Rattle at the four corners, around the place where you will be sitting or lying, and at the doorway. You can also burn sage or incense to create a sacred and pleasant environment. You can light a candle and keep it burning as long as you are sure that an open flame will not cause a fire. You may want to create a small altar that contains symbols of your intention for the journeywork.

Get yourself some blankets, pillows, eye shades, and other items that keep you comfortable. In my shamanic drumming circle at a local spiritual center, one of our members always wants the orange crocheted blanket to cover her. Its warmth and familiarity help her become comfortable, and also brings the energy of ritual to her preparation. Also, have water, your journal, and a pen nearby for afterward, so that you can easily reach the things you need to record your journey. Nothing is more irritating than to settle in, do the spiritual work, and then realize you left something outside the space. The aggravation can send the memories flying out of your head.

If you are doing trance work in your home, you will need to decide what to do about your pets, if you have any, and it will take some experimentation. Animals are attracted to this kind of energy and may want to help you or to participate. I have always been able to journey well with my animals in the journey space. Most often, they just settle down beside me and go to sleep or perhaps they are on their own journeys. Sometimes they participate in the journeys in ways that are serendipitous, wild, and appropriate, rather than becoming distractions or interruptions. The alternative is to lock them out of the space, although that does not work with my dogs, and I can tell you from experience that it's impossible to go into trance with persistent barking and whining outside the door.

Prepare Yourself

It is not necessary to do ritual baths or wear special costumes for this kind of work, but these preparations can be a nice enhancement to the spirituality of it. It is important to prepare your mind and your spirit for the journey ahead, so if special clothing and jewelry help you with this, then you should use them. Wearing clothing and jewelry is a way to prepare yourself from the outside in. Spend some time breathing deeply and connecting with the earth's energies. Ground and center yourself in a way that you are accustomed. One of the most typical ways to do this is to visualize roots growing from your tailbone or feet and moving deep into the ground. Pull the energy up from the earth and feel it dance and meld with the energy inside you. Then you. Then feel that combined energy move out into the universe from your crown; feel the Universe move to you and hold you in its embrace.

Mentally move from your daily life into a sacred mindset. You can do this in a variety of ways, and one of them is to use a distraction lockbox. You can envision your distractions, one by one, and place them in a box. Visualize the box being filled with your bills, taxes, co-worker relationships, or anything else that may inhibit you from journeying. Visualize the lid being firmly shut and locking the box. When you leave the space, you can open the box up and take all that stuff back into your life! But for the moment, it is out of sight and out of mind.

You can also smudge yourself with aromatic herbs such as sage (you will find more information on smudging in the section "Ceremony and Ritual"). Sage is cleansing and will dispel any lingering distractions. It will also move you into a mindset where you are ready to move into communication with the world of Spirit.

If you are new to shamanic journeywork—and even if you aren't—spend some time just listening to the drumbeat with no other intention other than to get into the rhythm and the sound. Use a tape or a drum and just get into the feeling of it. If you feel a random thought or anxiety come into your mind, recognize it and then move your attention back to the rhythm. Sometimes I just drum or listen to a drumming tape when I'm being a worrywart. The regular heartbeat rhythm attunes me to the greater Universe and my tiny worries don't seem so insurmountable.

I highly recommend that you do several sessions of drumming or rattling before you attempt other journeywork. For many people, this is a brand new concept and one that is wrapped up in the unknown and foreignness. That mystique can create a lot of anxiety about doing something well outside the realm of the familiar. If you regularly drum or rattle, then it becomes known to you and the movement into trance becomes less exotic and much more familiar.

And yes, do record your perceptions and feelings about this kind of drumming as well. Having a record will help you track your growth in power and wisdom.

Prepare Your Intention

All active spiritual work goes better with good preparation. If you go into a shamanic journey without focus, you will end, as we used to say when I was a kid, "any old where." If you focus your question and your intention, then you are more likely to have a successful journey. Being able to ask good questions is the key to getting good answers, and the beginning of our growth to wisdom. Questioning is a skill and an art—one that is easily learned.

Take some time to reflect on the situation for which you need answers or information. It is very appropriate to go to these worlds "just" to explore, but a clear intention is still necessary. Too many times, I've seen people in shamanic drumming circles come back from their journeys without a clear sense of what went on or the import of the meditation.

Your intention should be focused at least on one thing, but certainly not more than two. To say, "I'm going to journey on health, my job, and getting a new power animal," is too broad. Your spirit allies will probably do their best to show you things that have relevance to your quest, but the symbolism will probably be obscure. It's been my experience that these kinds of journeys speed up and become very confusing, and overwhelm me with a myriad of events, movement, symbols, and messages.

Your intention should not be so focused that it limits the ability of your spirit allies to guide you. How many times have you said about another person, "Well, I really can't tell her anything because she won't hear it?" This is the same concept. For example, if you state your intention about the need to switch jobs as, "I am going to the Lower World to seek wisdom about my new job that must be in my hometown and pay me at least $10 per hour more," it will really limit your vision of what could be possible for you, and what your spirit allies can show you.

You should be certain to state your intention clearly, and you should also state where you expect to find this information. "I am going to the Middle World to seek the spirit of the land my house sits on," is specific enough to give your guides and understanding of your desires while being broad enough so you don't limit their abilities. Your intention should also be flexible enough that you are open to surprising messages that may open new horizons for you.

Prepare Your Expectations

Sometimes our expectations of how we think our meditations should happen lead us to feelings of failure and disappointment. We live in a world where the moving image is ubiquitous; movies and television teach us erroneously how all moving images should be. Many of us, myself included, go into a meditation expecting it to unfold like we are watching a movie or television show—hopefully, there are no commercials or coming attractions movie trailers! Meditations of any kind rarely unfold like that. The important thing to remember is that we are active participants in our meditations, so even if the visual effect is like a beautifully staged movie, we are still actively participating in the meditation. Sometimes we *are* watching events unfold, but, more often than not, the meditation is happening to us.

As I said earlier, many people do not have clearly visualized journeys. I often do not; many of my journeys and meditations glide in and out of an atmosphere that is cloudy or dark. I've found it a useful technique to ask questions like, "What am I seeing here?" Other people I know experience combinations of sight, smell, and sound. More often than not, it is the feeling of the experience that resonates. I know that I am journeying because I feel it somewhere in my soul, my heart, and my gut. The important thing is to let go of your expectation that there is a right way and a wrong way to experience meditation. Let the understanding unfold and know that you are doing it absolutely the right way for you. Do not insist that your meditations be a certain way. You will be a lot calmer and more open, and wisdom will come to you more easily.

Sometimes we are disappointed because we feel that our journeys are not mystical enough. Perhaps, for example, when journeying for a power animal, you are approached by a mouse instead of a more impressive animal like a panther or a dolphin. All animals and teachers are important and have much to teach us if our expectations and preconceived notions do not get in our way. My partner, Mouse, has learned a lot from his power animal and, in turn, teaches the rest of us of the enormous power and wisdom a mouse power animal brings to situations.

And finally, when all the preparation is done, you are ready to journey. Take a deep breath, open your heart, and let yourself go. Your heart will beat in harmony with the drum, and you will dance into this wild magic!

Connecting to the Rhythm of the Universe

The circle began drumming together, or attempting to drum together. Everyone was drumming at a different rate, and at a different speed. Some were soft and some were loud. Suddenly and subtly, one person

became grounded and connected to her drum. Her drumming became
softer and more intent. Another person then connected with her drum,
and her rhythm began to harmonize with her neighbor's. Across the
room, another person became connected with his drum and beat in
unison with another. Gradually, everyone in the group became con-
nected with their own drum, and began drumming its voice. And like
a great choir, all the drums began harmonizing with each other. The
rhythms were different, but the power connected deep into the earth
and came out through each person's heart and hands.

It is a magical moment when the heart begins to beat in rhythm
with the drum. In groups of many drums, the drums will often
begin separately and eventually find a mutual beat and rhythm.
Hearts and blood also beat and throb in harmony with the tempo.
As previously mentioned, this phenomenon is called entrainment.
Mystically, entrainment is part of the process to which we are called
by the sacred beings we honor in our spiritual practices. All of us
long to dance with our Gods, and we can when we open our souls
to the beating heartthrob of the All-That-Is.

In any kind of spiritual practice, there comes a time when we
have to put the book down and just do it. This is a time to gather
up our anxieties and concerns and set them aside, and to gather
up courage, eagerness, and openness in order to give the magic a
try. Many of my early steps on the pagan path went just like that; I
read something in a book, and then gave it a whirl. Sometimes the
magic was great, and sometimes it needed some work—but I did it.
Being the writing and editing type, I tweaked whatever it was that I
was doing. So as you try the journeys and meditations in this book,
please adapt them to your personal needs and situations. Keep in
mind that there are basic principles that you should observe, but
everything else is open to your ability to adapt and transform.

The following is the journey that I mentioned earlier to connect with the rhythm of the drum. This is not a long journey, about ten minutes. You will be surprised, though, how much effort it will take to drum or rattle a steady beat for that long, if you are not used to drumming or rattling. It took me a while to find a posture I could maintain. That is why this is all about practice, practice, practice. Another helpful hint is to go ahead and set a timer for the time of meditation if you're going to drum for yourself. It feels like cheating, but it works. I have a terrible sense of time, and in the beginning I was very anxious about timing. Setting a timer really helped alleviate that anxiety. I could even set the timer in another room, and just hear the "ding" when it went off.

Tools Needed: Drum, rattle, or a recording of a drum or rattle. You will be beating a steady rhythm of the heart.

To Prepare: Prepare your ritual space, altar, and gather up items for comfort. Go into the space and settle yourself there. Become ready by grounding and connecting to the earth and by actively visualizing you anxieties put away from you. Call in any spirits that you wish to assist you. I always call in the energy of the directions, and the energy of my patron God and Goddess. There is no need to cast a circle at this point.

The Journey: Take three centering breaths. On the first inhale, breathe in calm, and exhale expectations. On the second inhale, breathe in power, and breathe out expectations. On the third inhale, breathe in wisdom, and breathe out anxiety. As the breath of the last exhale dissipates, begin your rattling or drumming. Keep on breathing and just feel the beat. Let all thoughts move in the rhythm and not linger. Keep it steady and resist the impulse to go faster. Just be in the rhythm.

The Ending: When you are finished, take three centering breaths and renew your connections to the earth. Take some time to write down your experiences, and feelings. Drink some water. Even if you think nothing happened, go ahead and record that you did this. Here is another time where you let go of expectations and just do it! It's been my experience that the wisdom can unfold as you start to write. If you are not a writer, go ahead and put pen, pencil, or crayon to paper. Doodle, draw, or do anything else that makes a record of the journey for you.

The Closing: Thank the drum, rattle, or even the recording for being a companion in this adventure. Thank any spirits that you called into your space. Take three cleansing breaths and you are done. Pick up, extinguish candles, and put the space back in order. This can be draining work, so go eat something or find a way to ground yourself in the everyday world again.

I suggest that you do this exercise many times so that the drumbeat becomes familiar. Once you do feel comfortable and familiar with this kind of drumming meditation, do not abandon it. I continue to just drum, integrating this kind of activity into a daily spiritual practice, because it is not only calming but an effective reminder of our connection to the sacred, a connection that is without words, thought, or work. Even experienced practitioners have difficulty meditating and journeying, and this simple exercise is a reminder that we all must have the heart of a beginner to learn the deepest wisdom.

The Magic of the Drum and the Rattle

The steady beat of the drum, lub-dub, lub-dub, lub-dub, tuned my body to the heartbeat of the Universe, and I sank into a deep trance.

It was winter, and I was in a cave deep in the earth. Firelight flickered and shadows danced on the wall, revealing ancient drawings of deep wisdom. I realized that there was drumming filling my awareness. I turned, and there was a circle of men, and they were drumming the rhythms of life and of the earth. They drummed rivers and streams, rocks, animals, people, and songs. All that is sacred was drummed by their hands. As I stood there and listened, my awareness expanded and I saw women dancing. They were dancing to the rhythms of life and of the earth. They danced the oceans, the stars, people, and animals. United in creation, the drum and the dance created a joyful, jubilant world. And then my guardian spirit gave me a push and I joined the dance.

The drum and the drumbeat are as ancient as we are. The drum tunes us to the rhythms of the world, teaching us that all wisdom, all healing, and all joy begins in harmony with the pulsing heartbeat of the Universe and the world that surrounds us. Different rhythms bring us different wisdom, and it all reaches into our beings through our bodies. Rhythm pulls us at a level of awareness where we are most primitive. Being primitive doesn't mean that we are ignorant or uncivilized, but that we shed the illusions and trappings of our socialization to become the creatures of the sacred. Our primitive selves are always there, moving under our civilized awareness and our everyday worries. Our primitive selves keep us connected to the sacred and to the universal harmony.

It all starts with the heartbeat: lub-dub, lub-dub, lub-dub. Sometimes in a circle, someone will start softly drumming the heartbeat. The drumbeat isn't really in the conscious awareness of the people in the circle, but still it begins. Discussion and speech begin to quiet, and people start to breathe in harmony with the drumbeat. The activity moves into a peaceful place, ready for the work of the circle. The people are in harmony, entrained to the vibrant pulse of the Universe. The drumbeat in shamanic journey-work is a specific rhythm, monotonous and consistent, of 180–220 beats per minute. The rhythm is steady and the drumbeat is loud enough to exclude distracting noises but not be the focus of attention.

To the shaman, the drum is both the vehicle for journeying and a magical companion on the journey. In many cultures, the drum has been called "The Shaman's Horse" because that is what the shaman rides into other realms, seeking power, wisdom, and healing. The comparison to a horse is not a casual one; it implies a relationship of mutual respect and responsibility. Just as a horse owner is responsible for the physical and emotional care and feeding of their horse, the shamanic practitioner builds a physical and emotional relationship with their drum.

Each drum has its own voice and personality, and so a practitioner may have a number of drums for different purposes. Often finding a drum brings the telling of a tale. Many years ago, I took my first shamanic drumming class in an intensive weekend retreat where we were told to bring drums and rattles if we had them. At the time, I was fairly new to every kind of alternative spirituality, having emerged from a very traditional religious background, and I didn't have those kinds of tools. But I did have enough of what I called "bogus occult experiences" to make me wary of spending a lot of money at the beginning on items and tools that I might not use again, to be stored away with my leather-bound Bible and old biblical commentaries.

But I didn't want to show up empty-handed, since the workshop had been highly recommended and I was a determined seeker, eager to find my spiritual home. So after looking at some beautiful expensive drums, I went to a toy store. I found a small, yellow drum with a popular storybook character drawn on it. It was actually a tambourine, and not the best choice for shamanic drumming, but I didn't learn that until later. The little toy appealed to me because yellow is my favorite color, and it was pretty. The workshop leader, who later became a respected teacher and friend, was amused by the drum and we used it in the group drumming situations. People ask me if I still have it, and I do. It's a beloved treasure. I am convinced that this humble little plastic drum helped me overcome my fear of moving into an unknown world, one that I had been taught was evil. She wasn't quite the shaman's horse for journeys, but a darling little pony that took me on the journey at the pace I needed to go.

The drums used for shamanic journeywork are frame drums and typically drummed with a beater. Some drums are double headed, meaning they have a skin covering on both sides. In those cases, one side has a deep sound, and the other is higher and lighter. There are drums covered in animal hide, and there are drums covered with inorganic materials. Some drums are mass-produced, while others are made individually. You can find drum-making workshops, or even use a wooden spoon and a plastic bowl. Finding your drum, or drums, is a part of a sacred process of becoming. Becoming a shamanic practitioner and becoming a Witch-Shaman.

The roundness of the drum reminds us of the circle, the symbol of our interconnectedness. The circle is eternal and reminds us that we are part of the infinite, like the chant says: "We are a circle within a circle/with no beginning, and never-ending." The past, present, and future become part of the unity of life when we hold our drums. The roundness of the drum tells us that we are part of the sacred world, and every time we beat the drum, we resonate with the wisdom of the sacred. The materials of the drum link us to the animals and trees that went into the construction of the drum itself. Synthetic drums also link us to the creative ingenuity of the universe that provides all ways to sing in unison and in harmony.

I did eventually buy a big grown-up drum! After taking the workshop and signing up to study with my teacher, I went to a local music shop. I was fortunate to live in an area where there was a lot of interest in world music, folk music, and traditional instruments. I was also lucky that day, since a local drum-maker had dropped off a lot of stock the week before. I spent a lot of time looking at the drums, feeling their drumbeats and just running my hands across their skin heads. It was a large investment for me, so I was careful not to make money an issue. Fortunately the store was fairly busy and the impressively knowledgeable clerks were working with other people, so I was left alone to listen to the spirit of the drums. When I took my chosen drum up to the cash register, the floor clerk praised me for my decision, saying I had bought a drum of real spirit. That drum was my primary shamanic drum for a long time. It is now used by my partner, Mouse, who treasures it and coaxes it to sing in new ways. Not only does each drum have its own voice, it will speak differently for different people and situations.

The drum I use now was a generous gift from Mouse. We were browsing in a drum shop, and this drum started calling to me. I recognized the pattern, since it is from a well-known manufacturer of drums, but it seemed to be stronger and more beautiful than others I had seen. It was expensive, so I didn't heed the call. But Mouse responded and asked me if I wanted him to buy the drum. I said no, because it was very expensive. He asked me if I liked it, and

I had to say yes. So he bought it for me, telling me he heard it clearly say it was for me and he was going to buy it despite my saying no. This is a doubly beloved drum because it was a gift from someone special, and because it has such a strong, beautiful voice; because of my feelings toward it, I don't allow anyone else but Mouse to use the drum.

Because I teach a lot, I usually have my wiccan tools and shamanic tools available for people to examine and feel. I think that you have to have the experiences of handling magical objects in order to feel the energies and energy effectively and wisely. This particular drum is an exception. The resonance we have together is very strong and individual, and I prefer not to have that relationship interrupted. This is not a judgment on the energies of others, but a desire to keep the communication between my drum and me clear, bright, and personal. As you walk in magical communities of any kind, you will learn a new kind of etiquette. One of the rules of good magical behavior is to ask permission of the owner of a tool before handling it. From drums to rattles to tarot cards to jewelry, magical practitioners attune themselves to their tools.

As you gather together the tools of shamanic practice, go about it with the intent to honor. Spend time with your drum, gazing at it, running your hands over it, and, of course, drumming it. Smudge it with burning herbs and incense. Talk to it. Tell it of your journeys. At some point, you may be led to know its name. You may be led to paint or decorate it. You may even be lead to build your own drum! Remember the voice of the drum is the voice of Spirit, and our connection to the harmony of the Universe. You will be building a relationship with this Drum Spirit, and, like all relationships, the drum needs time, care, and attention. It will need to work according to its nature, and that means it will need to sing.

In journeywork, the drum becomes an extension of ourselves, as not only the vehicle, but also the companion on our journey. It is the voice of the drum that leads us to the other realms, and calls us back to this world. The voice of the drum calls us to be magical and to work with the energies of magic, but also to come back with the wisdom we have gained. The vibrations of the drum remind us that energy is inherent in all things and that we are connected to all things through vibration, while the voice of the drum reminds us that we are always in harmony with the rhythms of the Universe, all creatures, and all spirits. The voice of the drum grounds us in relationship, and moves us outward into the realms of adventure.

The Rattle

The rattling began softly, chink-a, chink-a, chink-a, and was drowned out by the drums. The rattler was in deep concentration, and the rattling became louder. A drum started drumming the rattle's rhythm, and still the rattle became louder. Drums began to sing the rattle's song, until all became silent and the rattle continued on. When she came out of her trance, the rattler said, "I couldn't stop, I couldn't make it quiet. The rattle did what the rattle wanted to do!"

The rattle is another important tool in shamanic journeywork. I believe that we take it for granted because we associate it with babies and children's toys, underestimating the wisdom of a childlike connection to the world of Spirit. The rattle appeals to children not because it is childish, but because it speaks to our souls and to our primitive selves—the part of us that connects unconsciously to the worlds hidden from our view.

The rattle calls in the spirits from other realms and allows communication with them. Its sound is subtler and less demanding than the drumbeat. The rattle serves several purposes; first, it disrupts and dispels energies that attach to us and don't belong. By cleaning out this debris, you are open and you have a better ability to call to the world of spirit. Second, the rattle is a reminder that the Universe moves beyond duality and polarity into union. Rattles come from a variety of sources and constructions. Like the drum, it too is a symbol of unity. In many traditions, the rattle is the representation of the male life force, symbolized by the handle, uniting with the female creative energies, symbolized by the rounded part. The seeds, stones, crystals, and other objects inside the rattle are considered the voices of ancestors, both of blood lineage and of choice, who call to the spirits. Past, present, and future are united in the creation of a rattle. Every time the rattle is used, it sings of unity and calls to other spirits to join in that harmonious union.

I have a number of rattles, and one in particular stands out with personality and pizzazz. It is the rattle I always choose, and I rarely let others use it. Its name is Witchdancer, and I bought it at a gathering I attend yearly. It is hand-painted with dark colors and fiery symbols, and suits my personality and tastes. It has a subtle voice, not loud, but insistent and musical.

Believe it or not, a rattle's voice can be overpowering, so it needs to be used with compassion, attention, and intention. Its role of disrupting negative energies can spill over to disruption, and so careful attention is called for. As the person holding the rattle, you need to be aware of how its voice is affecting the people within the circle, and how it harmonizes with the drums and rattles also present. Using the rattle in a solitary ritual is a highly effective way to cleanse space, but you need to be careful that it doesn't chase away all the spirits. You need to let the rattle use its voice to sing its song. Like with the drum, you are building a relationship with the rattle.

The Spirit of the Drum

As I said earlier, each drum and rattle have a different voice, and it takes some time to find the right one for your personality and your intended use. The statement goes deeper than that, too, because each drum and rattle has its own spirit as well. With that spirit come a personality and sense of purpose. You may end up with a rattle that you use only for healing, and a drum that you use in all open drumming circles. It may take you some time to find the tool with the right spirit and personality, though in some cases, the spirit may come singing through. It all goes to developing a relationship with the percussion.

And then there is the overall Spirit of the Drum, the spirit that infuses everything with rhythm. It connects us soul to soul with the percussion instruments in our care, and it connects us heart and soul with the throbbing beat of the abundant and loving Universe. It is the spirit that called our ancient mothers and fathers, and it is the spirit that makes our Gods dance in joy and ecstatic union with us and with All-That-Is.

Connecting to Your Drum and Rattle

Each drum and rattle has its own voice, personality, mission, and message. As you work with your tools, you begin to develop a relationship with them, one based in mutual respect and love. The tools them-selves are inanimate objects, but you vitalize them with your inten-tion and continued work. The sinew, bone, skin, stone, and even synthetic materials will emerge, connect, and dance with you on your magical path.

In my professional life, I work with a lot of computer and me-dia technicians; there is an expression I've heard from them, and I'm not sure if it's from this particular area of the country, or a techno-speak that I've never heard before. What they say is, "parts is parts." I think it's charming, and it says to me that everything is a separate component part until we put it together and it becomes something important. Even parts that used to be something else become something new when put together in a different configura-tion. In many ways, our tools and our relationships with them are all separate parts until we put them together and make them something bigger. The energy that bonds us with our tools is our intention and our desire to work with the magical energies of the world.

Meditation and Exercise: Connecting to the Drum

This meditation and exercise can be repeated many times and will work with your rattles as well. It is not complicated, so do not make it hard work—it is a practice, so just practice it. Do, however, treat the practice respectfully. I am going to give you directions for con-necting to the drum, and you can adjust it for your other tools.

Prepare Yourself and Your Space: Prepare your space and your-self in the ways that you have established. Smudge yourself and your drum. Settle in, and don't forget to breathe and to breathe deeply. Pull in the energy of the earth from below and pull in the energy of the Universe from above. This exercise has several parts, and I recommend that you do each one separately several times, but you may also do them all at once.

Physical Connections: With eyes open, hold your drum so that you can run both hands over it. Feel the skin underneath your moving hands. Feel every inch of the skin, and just give yourself over to the feeling of it. Move to the rim, and do the same thing. Move to the reverse side of the drum and move your hands over that area as well. Give yourself over completely to the feel of the drum on your hands. You may want to move the drum over other parts of your skin, like the skin of your face. Completely give yourself over to the feeling of the drum on your skin.

When you feel it's time, open your awareness so that you hear what it sounds like to move your hands over the skin of the drum. Concentrate on what it sounds like to hear your hands move over the drum. Give yourself over entirely to the sound of your hands connecting with the drum.

When you feel it's time, open your awareness so that you smell the odors connected with your drum. Continue to run your hands over it and be aware of any smells that might emerge. You may find echoes of unexpected scents. Don't judge; just let the sensations come.

When you feel it's time, open your awareness to your sense of taste. I don't recommend that you lick your drum, so lick your lips and feel your taste buds inside your mouth awaken as your hands move over your drum. Be aware of anything that you might feel in your taste sensations.

Repeat this exercise with your eyes closed. You can also do this exercise, both eyes open and eyes closed, with your rattle or any other magical tool.

Gazing and Contemplation of Your Drum and Rattle

The instructions for this exercise are simple, and accomplishing it is the meditative work of a lifetime. Do this exercise with your drum and rattle separately. You can also use this technique with any of your magical tools.

In your sacred space, place your drum someplace where you can see it well, but it is just out of reach. Settle yourself comfortably in your space and breathe in deeply your connection to the earth and the Universe. When you are grounded and centered, gaze at your drum. Continue to contemplate the drum while breathing deeply. Allow your thoughts to still and center on the drum. When you are finished, thank the drum. Take a deep breath, ground and center, and then record your perceptions.

As you begin or deepen your shamanic practice, you will find that your tools, the drum and the rattle, are companions and allies in your work. Building a relationship with them and maintaining it is an absorbing and wonderful feeling, as well as necessary for you to have a deep and satisfying experience.

CHAPTER 3

Walking between the Worlds: Developing a Shamanic Practice

The lights were dimmed until only one candlelight flickered, and the drum started its throbbing heartbeat. What was an ordinary storefront became a land of mystery and magic. We closed our eyes and stated our intentions inside our heads. In my journey, I went to my place in nature, the maple tree, and climbed down the roots. I found myself in a tunnel that smelled like a forest after a rain. I felt safe and unafraid as I moved—or was I being moved by another power?—I came to an opening in the tunnel. I stood there at the threshold and looked out. I saw a different landscape than the flat, sandy farm in front of me. I saw lush, rich trees, an old growth forest in the summer. I walked forward . . .

The basic workshop of core Shamanism, as I was taught, and that I myself have taught, consists of several journeys to various places in nonordinary reality. This process has been enormously successful for many people all along the spectrum of age, gender, and economic class. There is a commonality of experiences for spiritual seekers. At the same time, these same factors, along with family background, race, and education, create the need for adaptability so that experience and culture are honored. Recently, I have tweaked, retooled, and changed my assumptions about how to teach basic shamanic practice.

This chapter contains my basic Shamanism workshop in the way that I have usually taught it, just as many teachers and practitioners teach it. My recent experiences have taught me that many people find the idea of Lower World journeys a little frightening, and so I often start them on Middle World journeys. We may spend a lot of time in the familiar environment of the Middle World before venturing into the Lower and Upper world. For people who are experienced with guided visualization, I use the inner shaman meditation found later in this chapter. You can work meditatively with your inner shaman and ask that guide to accompany you on your initial journeys.

Make your environment comfortable and cozy, and set out items of comfort such as blankets, pillows, and even stuffed animals. On my altar in our weekly shamanic journey group, I have a "salt doll," which is a little doll, just an outline of a female figure with yarn hair. The doll is stuffed with salt. You hold on to it and put all your negativity—fears, anxieties, anger, and the like—into it. Then, when you are finished, you give the doll a little shake and the salt cleanses away the negativity. One of the regular attendees used it while she learned to overcome her anxiety, and then made her own, which is part of her personal shamanic tool kit. Don't be afraid to use whatever it is you need to help you overcome the emotions that inhibit you, whether it is a treasured pillow, a stuffed bear, or a good luck charm. Whatever helps you is both important and good, whatever it may be.

As you approach this chapter, read it through and give the exercises a good, honest, sincere try in the order I have suggested. Don't give up after the first time, either. Keep on trying! If you find the work too inhibiting, start where you are comfortable. Call on your inner shaman and other guides you have found in your other practices, and ask for their assistance. May your journeys be blessed with wisdom and power.

Ceremony and Ritual

The room was full of chatter, as we were relaxing before the journeying began. It was at turns noisy and quiet as we waited for the work to begin. Our teacher was a small woman dressed in jeans and a sweater. She came to the center of the room and kneeled. From her tote bag she took a small woven blanket and lovingly spread it out. The room began to quiet. She brought out a candle and lighted it. The room quieted down some more. She placed a small object in each of the directions. Everyone in the room took a deep breath, and as she lighted the sage, the room fell silent and everyone was ready for ceremony. In a quiet voice she called in the spirits and guides of everyone present. In the silent room, we felt the energy shift and change. Power and magic had arrived.

In most cultures where shamans are honored and the concept of walking between the worlds is still understood and practiced within their society, the shamanic journey or healing is done with ceremony. Situating the journey within a ritual or ceremony is an important part of the process. It tells the spirit world and the human participants and onlookers that this is honored and important. Ceremony activates the parts of our minds and bodies to pay attention to the sacred. In a society where the sacred is not honored or considered, ceremony becomes even more important as a marker between everyday distractions and intentional, deliberate spiritual activity. Treating the process with reverence also helps us to recognize our own special, sacred abilities. Ceremony helps relieve us of our anxiety and sense of inferiority. Simple or complex, ceremony prepares us for the journey ahead.

In our weekly shamanic drumming circle, we have a simple ceremony that begins and ends each session. The framework of the ceremony is the same, which brings us a familiar comfort, and it is also special, so we become attuned to the energies around us. We begin by smudging each other around the circle. Smudging is an old tradition that spans many cultures. Herbs or incense is burned and the smoke is wafted over the person or item to cleanse, consecrate, and purify the person or item. Smudging helps bring people back into harmony with the Universe and to attune members of a circle to each other.

Different herbs and herbal combinations have different properties, strengths, and meanings. Sage is used to purify and cleanse, and its scent is energizing and invigorating. Lavender is a universally loved herb that is inspirational and promotes harmony, healing, and happiness. Experiment with herbs and incenses to find what works best for you. If you are working in a group, be sure that no one has an asthmatic condition or allergy. In those cases, essential oils work very well. A good cleansing combination is lemon and water, spritzed around the circle or room. I don't recommend spritzing other people in the face, but you could sprinkle or asperse them or the air around them with this mixture.

Then, we co-create the circle by calling in the energies of the directions, starting with the direction of the season. So in the spring we start with the East, in the summer we start with the South, in the fall we start with the West, and in the winter we start with the North. The times are guided by celestial movements, the equinoxes, and solstices. After calling in the cardinal directions, we call in the energy of Below and Above. We follow by calling in the affinities and energies that we feel in the air. Then we honor each one's sacred nature by bowing to each one in turn. We then do our journeywork in sacred space.

After we are finished with our journeying and sharing, we close the circle. Closing the circle is in symmetry to the opening. I call it, "doing it all backwards," so in the spring, we close the circle starting in the North, then to the West, then to the South, and then to the East. We then close Below and Above. Here is a sample opening and closing for a springtime ceremony, adapted for a solitary ceremony, but can be easily adapted for a group.

Opening: In the opening, each of us taps into the feelings we have that day about that direction. Be creative and alert to your own spiritual needs and to what surrounds you.

I call the spirits and creatures of the East, of springtime, and the fresh breezes of change. Imagination and the mind. Fresh buttercups and daisies, the smell of soil just overturned, songbirds and vitality. Intuition and joy, vigor and growth. Spirits and creatures of the East hail and welcome!

I call on the spirits and creatures of the South, of hot summertime. Salsa, coyote, trickster, play, persistence, and passion. Heat, burning sun, willpower, power, and accomplishment. Noon day picnics, ants, and flies. Choice, determination, and dragons. Spirits and creatures of the South, hail and welcome!

I call on the spirits and creatures of the West, of the sunset and the waves of longing. Mermaids, falling leaves, and the autumn harvest. Mystery, magic, and the heart. Sensual delights, chocolate, and the receding wave. Swimming creatures and deep rest. Spirits and creatures of the West, hail and welcome!

I call on the spirits and creatures of the North, of dark midnight and the deep earth. Mountains, bears, and wolf. Deep snow-covered paths and smoke curling out of chimneys. Stability, foundation, death, and rebirth. Hibernation, wisdom, and sleep. Spirits and creatures of the North, hail and welcome!

I call on the spirits and creatures and spirits of Below. Roots, dirt, soil, and the creepy-crawlies. Mother Earth, the core, and power of being. Hidden treasures and messages. Spirits and creatures of Below, hail and welcome!

I call on the spirits and creatures of Above. Teachers, infinity, illumination, and celestial beauty. Wisdom, laughter, darkness, and joy. Spirits and creatures of Above, hail and welcome!

Closing: I believe that the spirits and creatures of these realms help us because they want to, and because in doing so they gain blessings and power. It is a partnership. I usually include "Go with my thanks and my blessings" to honor their work with me. I am grateful that I get to live this life of spirit, and they are my companions on the path.

Spirits and creatures of the North: Thank you for your presence and thank you for stability and foundation. Thank you for the reminders that we are all one with the soil, rocks, and mountains. Go with my thanks and my blessings. Hail and farewell!

Spirits and creatures of the West: Thank you for your presence and thank you for the deep longing of the soul. Thank you for the water that buoys us up, and the water that cleanses our souls. Go with my thanks and my blessings. Hail and farewell!

Spirits and creatures of the South: Thank you for your presence and thank you for the playful humor. Thank you for the hot summer sun and the persistence and passion to get the work done. Go with my thanks and my blessings. Hail and farewell!

Spirits and creatures of the East: Thank you for the freshness and vitality of springtime. Thank you for discernment, intuition, and joy. Go with my thanks and my blessings. Hail and farewell!

Spirits and creatures of Below: Thank you for the grounding and roots. Thank you for the creepy-crawlies and the little creatures. Thank you for the core of our being, burning bright and hot. Go with my thanks and my blessings. Hail and farewell!

Spirits and creatures of Above: Thank you for the vision of the infinite. Thank you for teachers and the beauty of the Heavens. Go with my thanks and my blessings. Hail and farewell!

Ceremony and preparation does not need to take a long time. But do take the time. It tells the spirits with whom you are working that you honor them and honor yourself. You step away from your everyday world and its concerns into a circle where the sacred world awaits you with arms open in an embrace.

Basic Journeys for the Shamanic Student

My first shamanic drumming class was held in an empty store, a very nice store with wooden floors and plain walls. It was deep evening, so the room was lit by candlelight. There was an animal skin set out with objects on it. None of us knew each other, so there wasn't much conversation other than the usual small talk associated with a new class, although my little yellow drum was greeted with some affectionate laughter. The teacher had us pause and breathe. Then she picked up her drum and began to drum. Everyone else began to drum. I couldn't help myself as I joined in and felt my spirit soar into the drumming. I could hear singing, but wasn't sure from who or what. Suddenly, this nice empty store became a magical place where the ancestors came and power sat down to play the drum.

To begin work as a shamanic practitioner, the seeker undertakes a series of short journeys to find power allies and teachers and to explore the terrains of the three worlds.

Journey One:	Journey to the Lower World to familiarize yourself with the landscape
Journey Two:	Journey to the Lower World to find a power animal
Journey Three:	Dancing your power animal
Journey Four:	Journey to the Upper World to find your teacher
Journey Five:	Journey to the Middle World

Even when learning and experimenting, it is important to pay attention to the space where the journeywork will occur. Arranging and cleaning the space is an important part of an effective journey to the worlds of Spirit. Cleansing the space by rattling or with herbs such as sage, creating an altar, and calling in the spirits of the directions of this world are all customarily done in preparation for a journey. The room should be darkened, the phone taken off the hook, and other distractions minimized. Preparation and ceremony are ways of honoring the work that we do and honoring the spirits and creatures that journey with us.

It is useful to do some preliminary work before starting the shamanic journeying, because often a seeker may be nervous or anxious about embarking on journeys to unknown worlds of consciousness, particularly since our culture teaches us that these worlds are Hell and Heaven. Added to that attitude is the presence of drums and rattles as meditation aids, which are tools that are unfamiliar to many people. Adding even more anxiety to the process are the stories of shamans of exotic or remote aboriginal cultures, which can be intimidating for some. These combined factors can create a level of anxiety that inhibits effective trances.

Everyone has the capability to be a shaman inside of them; it is simply a matter of choice and training. Absolutely everyone can be a powerful shamanic practitioner if they choose to, but a good way to start is with a meditative technique that is familiar, such as a guided meditation. The following meditation provides the seeker with a spirit ally before they begin their journeys into an unfamiliar cosmos. Each person can tap into their own inner power and divinity to find their inner shaman. When I did this meditation for the first time, I discovered that my inner shaman was a manifestation of my patron Goddess. In this guise, she is full of color and light. She dances and swirls around me to remind me that to journey is to be active and ecstatic.

Guided Visualization:
Finding Your Inner Shaman

Ground and center yourself. Take a long, deep, centering breath and let go of any expectations you may have. Take a second long, deep, centering breath and let go of any anxiety you may have. On the next inhale, breathe in peace and breathe out peace. Again, breathe in peace and breathe out peace. As you continue to breathe deeply, close your eyes. Find yourself in your favorite space outdoors. It is safe, warm, and peaceful.

Walk around this special place of yours, drinking in the colors and the sights. Breathe in the smells and listen to the sounds of your favorite place. Find somewhere to sit in your favorite place. Make yourself comfortable there as you breathe in and breathe out. Remember all the good memories and feelings of this wonderful place. As you relax, you begin to hear a rhythm and a beat. You might sway a little bit to the rhythm because you know that this is the heartbeat of this, your favorite place. As you feel the pulse of this place, know that it is the heartbeat of Mother Earth. Listen to this rhythm. Feel it in your bones and in your blood. Your blood begins to pump in unison with this rhythm. Your heart begins to beat in unison with this rhythm.

Now you stand in this wonderful place. You stretch yourself straight and tall, feeling the energy of the place fill you from head to toe. As you breathe deeply, you look around and notice a small bonfire a little distance before you. You can hear a steady drumbeat and you know there are people gathered around the fire. You walk there, toward this bonfire.

When you get there, you realize that this is a special gathering. You see lots of people and hear them singing, laughing, and telling stories. You feel the drumbeat and see that the people begin to dance around the fire. As you watch, you notice the people around the fire, dancing, laughing, and singing.

One of the people attracts your attention as someone special. Notice, and think why that person is special. As you watch, the person notices you, too. Breaking away from the dance, the person moves toward you, reaches out, and holds both your hands. The person looks deep into your eyes and the two of you see each other on every level: heart to heart; soul to soul; eye to eye. You know each other. This is your inner shaman. Notice all you can about your inner shaman.

As you are taking all you can, your inner shaman pulls you into the dancing. You move wildly among all the people, absorbing their joy and delight. Around the fire you dance. Dance, dance, dance.

The dancing stops; you and your inner shaman stand together, looking into each other's eyes. In your hand, your inner shaman places a gift—a talisman for your seeking and your journeywork. Say thank you and turn to go back to your special place. Return to your special place and, with a deep breath, feel the rhythm of that place. Take another breath, and find yourself back in the here and now. With another breath, open your eyes.

When you are back in ordinary reality, commemorate and express the wisdom of your journey by writing it, drawing it, or dancing it. Begin to build a relationship with your inner shaman. Draw the talisman you were given. You may well find a physical world counterpart for your altar and sacred space. As you begin to do journeywork, keep an image of that talisman on your altar or close at hand while you trance.

Creatures and Spirits of the Other Realms

As the drumbeat starts its heart rhythm, I move to my place in nature with the intention of going to the Upper World. I call my power animals to me: "Who's here?" I ask. Instantly, I feel Polar Bear's massive and comforting presence. Wolf nudges my left hand, and Flamingo flies gracefully pink around my head. I climb on Polar Bear's back and we take off, up through the branches of the tree. We move through the clouds and suddenly we are in water. Polar Bear loves to come up through the fountain into the Upper World. He tosses me off his back and I catapult onto an outdoor pavilion. I land gracelessly on all fours. I get up and look around. I see a garden, and a woman out there, hoeing neat rows of beans. I walk over and she hands me a rake and a hoe. Uh-oh, I thought, I have some work to do.

In the shamanic practice, our allies and teachers come to us in the shape of animals and in human form. Both humans and animals can appear to us in the Lower and Upper Worlds. I've also met with my teachers and power animals in the Middle World, during dreams, walks, and meditations. They are linked to us by their choice and by our choosing. It is most typical to encounter our power animals in the Lower World and our human form teachers in the Upper World. What is right and important is to know that your experiences are authentic and there is no right and wrong. As you begin to walk this path, you will find that your dance and your experiences will vary with the rhythms of your own life.

Power Animals

I went to my place in nature and started to climb down the roots. I found the tunnel, and quickly found my way out into the Lower World. Boy, did the landscape look different this time! I could hear steel drums playing calypso, and see houses perched up on cliffs. I could hear the ocean, and waves crashing on the shore. The calls of exotic birds were all around me. I found myself on a bicycle, riding around this island seeking something I couldn't find. Finally, two birds presented themselves to me, and told me they were new power animals. One was a parrot with bright red feathers; the other was a pink flamingo. I must admit, I thought that the world of Spirit was playing a tacky joke on me; it wasn't until I saw a program on TV that I realized the beauty, power, and grace of the flamingo. They are more than just plastic lawn ornaments!

Over the years, Parrot taught me how to squawk so I could be heard, and Flamingo taught me to look harder underneath my assumptions to find real meaning. Flamingo also paved the way for Heron, and wading deep into the waters of mystery.

There is a lot of terminology where animals and magical practices are concerned. Guardian spirits, power allies, power animals, totems, and familiars are all terms used in relationship to animals and spiritual paths.

In many ways, power allies, guardian spirits, and power animals share the same kind of energy, but their roles and relationship to you, the seeker, is different, a nuanced and subtle difference at that. Guardian spirits are the spirits that are with us throughout our whole lives. They may manifest themselves as animals, angels, teachers, or other beings. Their role is to protect you and guide you through this lifetime. This protection and guidance may come in the form of teaching, rescue, or that flare of good luck you seem to have for no apparent reason. You will find that they accompany you on your journeys, and they may feel like power animals as well as guardians. I have Polar Bear as my guardian spirit. This was a power animal that was retrieved for me by a classmate in my first class. I immediately resonated with this powerful, swimming, and playful bear. Polar Bear has been with me in every journey that I have ever taken, and often shows up in other kinds of meditations.

I have other guardian spirits that are not typical according to most writers and teachers of shamanic practice. I think it is because I am a witch, and though I didn't claim that title until twenty or so years ago, I have been a witch since I was a little girl. In this case, my guardian spirit is Ariadne of Crete, who is also my patron Goddess. She has been in my life in this form since junior high. In myth, her husband is Dionysus, and he is also my guardian spirit, teaching me about ecstasy and the ability to experience joy and pleasure without guilt.

When Ariadne serves as guardian, her energy is slightly different than when she is working with me as my patron and as my inner shaman. I know it sounds confusing. We as humans try to make sense of things in categories and linear ways, when the world of Spirit is not bound by our linear thinking about time and space. We do the best we can to understand and explain, but it is part of the mystery to experience the unexplainable with an open heart and soul.

Power animals are the creatures that assist you in your journeys. They serve, not as servants, but as partners in discovery. Most people have one or two power animals that stay with them throughout most of their lives, with other animals called power allies that stay with them during a particular period in their lives, or to help them through a situation. My primary power animal is Polar Bear. He has been with me in every journey and every healing session. I have had others that have stayed for a long time, but do not have the same resonance that Polar Bear has for me.

Power allies are power animals that come into our lives for a short time to help us through a particular challenge or a difficult period in our lives. I once had a power ally, Skunk. At the time, I was working in at a job that was characterized as emotionally toxic. While I had good friends there, the culture of the workplace was one of anger, jealousy, and betrayal. When I got promoted, instead of celebrating, most of my friends became backstabbing enemies. Skunk came to me when I was adjusting to my new role, and helped me find the people who were stinkers and were skunking me. I eventually left that job for a better one. I never made the connection until a friend said, many years later, "Nothing will make you leave a place faster than a skunk." After awhile, I realized that

Skunk had moved on, but I remember him with a lot of gratitude and affection.

When you connect with a power animal, you also connect with their magic on a spiritual and species level. You connect with the spirit of Skunk, and the spirit of Wolf. That is not to say that they don't have individual personalities and ways of relating to you, because they do. But you also connect with them on a powerful, mythic, universal level. Always, your connection as you experience it is the truth.

When you have a power animal, build a relationship with it. Surround yourself with images including statues, pictures, pocket tokens, and, like I do, a screen saver on your computer. Research the natural behavior of the animal, including nature books and nature television programs. Remember, you are the authority in this situation, so if something you read or find out about the symbolism and behavior doesn't fit the behavior of your power animal in nonordinary reality, it is because that animal is telling you something you need to know, and it is right. Many people I know have power animals that smoke or demand an exchange of tobacco. My power animals swim, fly, and dance, even though their natural-world counterparts do not. Even though these things don't occur in ordinary reality, within the context of the journey, it makes perfect sense.

Whatever you do, enjoy the journey and open your heart and spirit. These are relationships built in love and harmony. You will find that these beings are with you at your finest moment and your darkest hour. They love you, they help you, and most of all, they remind you that none of us is alone and separate in the Universe. We *are* all connected.

We were journeying in the Middle World to see if there were people who needed assistance to cross over from this plane of existence to the land of the dead. I was nervous about it, to say the least. The drumbeat began its heart rhythm and I sank deep into trance. I found myself on a rainy street in Baltimore or Washington, I couldn't tell which. It looked familiar, Baltimore, I thought, but it could have been either place. I felt Falcon flying around me, and Parrot was perched on my shoulder. Wolf nudged my left hand, and Polar Bear was to my right. I had a sense there were other animals around me, ones that I hadn't met yet but who wanted to assure me that this was possible and I could do the task set for me. The light from the streetlights and the headlights illuminated the puddles in eerie ways. There was a car wreck with ambulances and police cars, their lights creating prisms in the puddles and raindrops. A short distance away, the driver, dead I could tell, was watching all the commotion with a puzzled expression. As we walked closer, he turned and looked at us. "Boy, lady," he said. "You sure have a lot of animals around you." I smiled and I could feel the mirth of the animals around me. And we began the work of helping this man.

Teachers

I was doing a series of journeys to the chakras, and this one was to the solar plexus chakra—the power chakra. I had trouble starting out, and then I ended up in a street fair. People were dressed in costumes like in the musical Kiss Me Kate. There was a sword swallower and a fire-eater, and lots of laughter and fun, and I heard music and the voice of a wonderful singer. I went over to watch, and realized it was *a singer I admired, Howard Keel, who had died the week before. He spotted me and came over, and looked at me and sang, "Bless your Beautiful Hide." I was very happy and grinning widely. He started to sing another one of his signature songs, and I said, "I've really got to go on this journey." He smiled and said, "You are in the journey right now. Enjoy each moment." He kissed me on the cheek and said, "I'll be singing for you." I went on with the solar plexus journey much more joyful and centered—the rhythm had changed. The Sun card in the Tarot reminded me that living in the sunlight is living in joy. Singing songs that we love and being sung to is joyful living.*

We all have teachers in the realms that overlap with ours. Most often our teachers appear in the Upper World and they appear to us in human form because that is what we can understand. They will appear to us as folk heroes, deities, admired people who have died, and so on. Like power animals, we have one or two who stay with us for a long time, even a lifetime, and then ones who show up once, like in the story above, or during a period of our life. The journey above came at a time when I was anxious about the events in my life and having trouble staying focused. While the journey may seem a little odd, it had a profound effect on me and on the work I was doing at the time. It spoke to me in the images, sounds, and people that resonate inside me at the deepest levels. That is what all journeywork will do.

Sometimes our teachers are beloved figures, and other times they are people who challenge us. In one of my classes, a classmate went to the Upper World to find her teacher, and Jesus appeared before her. My classmate was appalled and completely rejected the idea that Jesus could be a teacher for her, and so she therefore rejected the teacher. Undeterred, the world of Spirit found another teacher for her; this time, it was a woman's voice, disembodied, and coming from a Grecian temple. Her reaction to the idea of Jesus as her teacher taught me a couple of things. One was not to expect that all teachers will be exactly what we want and to look deeply at the teachers that come our way; second was that the world of Spirit wants to reach out to us, and will forgive us for rejecting their gifts and will still continue to teach and to help us. Because of that, I was able to accept Jesus as one of my teachers and healing guides when he emerged in an Upper Realm journey a few years later.

I have two teachers, or maybe it could be better described as two sets of teachers. The first teacher and the one I speak to most often is a woman, always working in a garden. She presents herself as either a toddler, a middle-aged woman barefoot and in coveralls, or as an older woman with long gray hair. Each form teaches me different things, and I am sure they are part of the same woman, just at different ages. She (or they) has yet to tell me their names, but it never seems important to ask. She usually gives me tasks to perform and work to do, from which I construct my own wisdom.

My second teacher is a man who lives in what might be described as a stately building, not unlike the important government buildings found in Washington, D.C. I'm familiar with those buildings because I spent a good portion of my life in the suburbs of D.C. Sometimes it looks like one of the two buildings of the Library of Congress, and sometimes it looks like the Supreme Court building. I always visit him in a large study with a huge domed ceiling made of glass so we can see outside and into the Heavens. He is surrounded by books and informational technology. His technology has changed over the years and is always up-to-date. He has shown himself as Merlin, Jesus, and a nameless God of the Woods. He always tells me the wisdom I need to know. It's usually a case where I've been too dense or involved to see the wisdom right in front of me. My teachers are very patient with me, and speak to me in ways that I can hear and understand.

Journeying to the Lower World

The words "Underworld" and "Lower World" are often used interchangeably and refer to the realms that are beneath our feet. The Underworld is not physically under the ground, but located in the parallel places that overlap ours. To get there, we journey downward. The Lower World is where our power animals reside and where our animal-like natures can receive information. It is a place for exploration of physical ailments, bodily issues, intuition, and psychic development. The Lower World is instinctual and a place where we can find earthy guidance. Things that can occur there can be funny, violent in a cartoon-like fashion, symbolic, or literal. As previously mentioned, this does not correspond to the Hell of mainstream religions, but rather to those entities that connect us bodily to this world and to the other worlds. Often issues such as health, sorrow, depression, and death make the Lower World seem like a hellish place; however, the ultimate goal of all the worlds is harmony with universal energies, and these are issues that need attention. It can also be terrifying because the landscape looks very much like our everyday world.

To journey to the Underworld, pick a real place in nature that goes down into the earth. It can be the root of a tree, a cave, a well, or a hole in the ground. It should be a real place that you know of. I use the roots of one of the maple trees outside my mother's house. That house belonged to my grandparents, and my favorite uncle planted two maples with a teaspoon when he was a little kid. I know those trees quite well because I have climbed them, daydreamed in a hammock beneath them, and been shaded by them as I visited with family. Recently, my mother had to have the trees removed, but the roots still remain. I've used them so often in journeywork that they now exist on the astral planes. Another place I use is a cave I visited once but remains vibrant in my memory and in my mind's eye. Other practitioners use places that they have never experienced in the physical world, but my teachings and experiences tell me that the places you have touched and have touched you work best.

As you go downward into the earth, you will enter into a tunnel. You will journey through the tunnel until it opens up into the Underworld. The landscape may change with each visit; there will often be physical reminders of this world in that landscape.

Lower World Journey Basics

- Pick an actual place in nature that goes downward into the ground.

- State your intention clearly and succinctly three times. You might say, "I am going to the Underworld to observe the landscape."

- Follow that place downward into a tunnel.

- Follow the tunnel through an entryway into the Lower World/Underworld.

- When the signal to return is sounded, return the same way you came.

As you begin your adventures with this kind of meditation, please be sure to follow the suggestions in the earlier chapters. Let go of your expectations and preconceived notions about what should to happen, and let the journeys unfold. Relax into the experience. Let go of anxieties and know that each of us perceives the wisdom on trance in different ways. Know that what you are hearing, seeing, smelling, feeling, or touching is a valid experience. Understand that you will see the journey unfold in your own unique way, and let go of any expectations you may have that about the way your journeys will look.

Even though there is nothing that can do you real harm, sometimes the images and journeys can be alarming. If you become too scared to continue, just raise your arm in the air, sit up, and shake yourself out of the trance. There is nothing wrong with that. Be sure that if you come out of a trance in that way, you do some grounding and caretaking of yourself afterward. Write down the experience and what alarmed you. Find ways to alleviate that anxiety. Be sure that you are centered and grounded, and use the grounding meditation in the appendix of this book if you need guidance. Take care of yourself.

Having one bad experience, either because it doesn't meet your expectations or you found something unsettling, does not mean that you will always have bad experiences. Try again and breathe in a determination to greet each experience with joy.

Journey One:
Journey to the Lower World to Familiarize Yourself with the Landscape

This journey is to familiarize you with the process of journeying to the Underworld. It will be a relatively short journey. The drum will beat rhythmically as you give yourself over to it. Go on the journey, and when the drum signals a return, come back the way you came—up through the tunnel, and up through your place in nature.

When you enter the Underworld, you may be greeted by animals and other beings. Your purpose is to become familiar with the landscape; another journey will aid you in forming relationships with the creatures. Be sure to talk to them politely.

You may find that your power animal will greet you immediately and insist on taking you places. Go with it, and let it happen. If you find the journeying difficult or outside your experience, know that this is a typical reaction and don't get upset about it. For many people, especially if you are trying this on your own, shamanic journeying is a new, even foreign, experience. You can do it, but it is a skill gained through practice and patience. It is important to not judge yourself if you don't have an A+ experience the first time. Most of us have to keep on trying! For this journey, it is important to let go of your expectations and remember that it is your intention to go to the Lower World and become familiar with the landscape.

Journey One Basics

- Go to your place in nature.

- State your intention three times: "I am going to the Lower World to become familiar with journeywork and the Lower World."

- Go downward into a tunnel and through the entryway into the Underworld.

- Observe the terrain, its creatures, and any other information that may come your way; have conversations with any friendly beings that you meet.

- When the drum signals to return, follow the same pathway back to the starting point.

When you return, take some time to ground and center yourself. Breathe deeply and connect yourself to Mother Earth. Write about your journey. Even if you feel that you didn't see anything, start writing because you may find that as you write more information comes to you. If you are journeying with a group, take some time to talk about your individual journeys. As you go around the circle, let each person talk of their journey without interruption, allowing them to draw their own interpretations and conclusions about the symbolism of the journey. After the first debriefing, a deeper discussion and analysis is often helpful.

You may wish to repeat this journey more than once so that you feel comfortable with the process and your own style of journeying. Understanding how you experience this kind of meditation will go a long way in helping you have good, strong experiences. It is similar to attending wiccan rituals when you first start out; once you get to know the ritual framework and knowing what goes where and what comes next, you are then better able to feel the magic and the power of the work being done.

Journey Two:
Journey to the Lower World
to Find a Power Animal

The second journey is to the Lower World to find a power animal; an animal who will act as guide, ally, and friend. The process of the journey will be the same, except this time you will walk farther into the terrain of the Lower World. As you do, you will encounter creatures that may or may not talk to you. How will you know if a particular creature is your power animal? There are a variety of ways: the creature will identify itself to you; it will answer in the affirmative if you ask, "Are you my power animal?"; or, you will see it a number of times (often three is considered the magical number). In any of these cases, there is usually little doubt that the creature is an ally for you.

Traditionally, seekers were told not to regard insects as potential power animals. I have found that insects and invertebrate creatures such as worms, bees, or snakes can be important power animals for people, particularly witches. The affinities that these creatures have with various Goddesses of the world, or the creatures' sacred role in our own natural world, make them good teachers and power animals for witches. It is important, however, not to retrieve a power animal that is menacing toward or bares its teeth at you.

These creatures are not power allies. Creatures with that kind of behavior are usually the bearers of messages and warnings, not power animals.

One of the anxieties people have is that they won't get a power animal on the first try. That certainly happens, and you may find that afterward an animal may manifest itself to you repeatedly, either in the natural world or through media or discussions. Be open to many possibilities. If you continue to journey and to seek, you *will* find a power animal. Another option is to have an experienced shamanic practitioner retrieve a power animal for you, using a special shamanic technique.

After you have journeyed and retrieved a power animal, the drum will signal you to return to ordinary reality. As you wake back to this world, hold an image of the animal in your cupped hands, and with an indrawn breath, place that animal into your aura, at your heart. Be prepared for a relationship full of blessings and adventure!

Journey Two Basics

- Go to your place in nature.

- State your intention three times: "I am going to the Lower World to find a power animal."

- Go downward into a tunnel and through the entryway into the Lower World.

- Walk into the Lower World and observe and talk to the animals there; greet your power animal.

- When the drum signals to return, follow the same pathway back to the starting point.

- As you sit up in ordinary consciousness, hold an image of the animal in your cupped hands.

- With an indrawn breath, place that animal in your aura at your heart.

When you return to this world of consciousness, take the time to write down your journey, and draw your power animal. If you are journeying in a group, talk about the journey and the power animal. Be ready for magic to happen.

In the days following your journey, you may find that the animal shows itself to you in surprising and funny ways. If the animal is native to where you live, you may see it more often than you usually do, or people in your life will start telling you stories of their encounters with your animal. Don't dismiss these as coincidences! If the animal is not native to your area, you might find pictures in magazines, on television, or on your computer. When Flamingo manifested as my power animal for a time, I kept running across magazine articles and, once, a wonderful documentary of this beautiful bird. Never mind that pink flamingos are ubiquitous items for knick-knacks, T-shirts, and other popular culture items! Those kept coming into my life repeatedly as well.

Your animals seek a relationship with you. Take some time to research your animal, make collages, and collect pictures of your animal. Incorporate the animal into your spiritual and magical practices. By consciously building knowledge and incorporating the animal into your life, you build a relationship that will help you in your journeys within nonordinary reality. Your animal will continue to show its own unique personality and abilities—my polar bear flies and can row a boat—to teach you lessons and bring you messages. Keep yourself flexible as you embrace this shamanic work with your mind, heart, and soul.

Journey Three: Dancing Your Power Animal

The room was dark and the drumbeat started. I was feeling self-conscious about dancing around everyone, but I closed my eyes and took a deep breath. I started to dance what I thought were the movements of a polar bear. Suddenly, I felt another's energy within me, and I got on all fours and lumbered around. I stood on all fours and roared . . . and then I felt like I was swimming. The water was cold, but I was protected by a layer of fat and fur. I had to grin to myself and think, "It really is true—flabby but graceful!" I moved into the rhythm of the drum and I could feel myself merge with the power and grace of this large animal.

The third journey in this sequence is a Middle World journey, and you will stay on this plane of existence. I know of many people who skip this journey; however, I feel this is an important part of developing an understanding of the animal who is your guardian and with whom you will be building a partnership and relationship. Dancing the power animal will fill your body with the spirit of that animal and imprint it on your body, down to the cellular level. You will feel it in your bones and experience it as a union. Many of the dances of indigenous peoples mimic the behavior of animals, often the totems of their family or clan. By interpreting the animal behaviors with our human bodies, we invite the spirit to become a part of our lives and our daily activities.

Treat this as a festive occasion, a much-anticipated party, where your favorite people are coming to cut loose and have some fun. Dress in clothes that make you want to dance, and wear the jewelry of your animal or of your spiritual path. I used to be very resistant about dancing, being self-conscious about my body and how I looked, but dancing my power animal was different. I was filled with that spirit and one of the things I admire about the polar bears I had seen at the zoo, swimming in the water, was that they were "flabby but graceful." Dancing my power animals with only my dogs to watch gave me grace. Dancing my power animals helped me overcome self-consciousness and so I dance.

Journey Three Basics

You begin by rattling the directions, and then the drumming takes over as you dance. You can have someone drum for you or use a drumming tape. Begin by rattling in the east, the place of dawn and new beginnings. Rattle and invite the spirit of the animal to join you in the dance, with words such as, "Great Polar Bear, my guide and guardian, come dance with me. Fill me with your spirit and join me!" Rattle at every direction, calling to the spirit to join you. Keep rattling until the rhythm is felt in your body, turn on the drumming tape, and begin to dance the animal. You will find that this happens naturally—just let it happen. Don't worry about doing it right, or how you look. It is fun. Move your body as you are led to move. Let go and dance!

Journey Four:
Journey to the Upper World
to Find Your Teacher

I was pulled up to the Upper World on a wire, a bit like a circus trapeze artist moving upward to the trapeze. I twisted and turned as I went upward through the cloud cover. The next thing I knew, I was in a circus, riding the elephant, who happened to be the God Ganesha. The scene then morphed, and I was riding a horse and jumping through hoops. The Ringmaster was my teacher, and instead of coveralls, she was dressed in a red coat and top hat. She was calling the shots, and I was following them. It was a very complicated scene of several rings and performances, but everything went along flawlessly, even though I couldn't see the pattern. I could smell popcorn and hear calliope music. I decided to stop trying to see the pattern and go along for the ride. I relaxed and it became an effortless and beautiful performance. "Excellent," I heard her say to me. "And now relax into the hard work you have to do in your life."

The Upper World is above us in those realms that intersect and overlap, and each one of us is a point of intersection, of union. Some writers on modern Shamanism, especially those trained as psychologists, will say that we are really journeying into our own imagination and spiritual realm. That is indeed true, at least in part. The cosmos of the shaman is shaped by the journeyer, but while each of us has a personal view of the terrain, there are worlds that extend beyond ourselves.

We journey to the Upper World for greater wisdom about our life goals, about things concerning our intellect, mind, feelings, and emotions. We may go there for wisdom about both past and present lives. While the Lower World provides wisdom about our body and its heath and ills, the Upper World may provide us with healing wisdom on the spiritual level. Even as this is said, remember that these "rules" are the perspectives of other journeyers, and your experiences may vary. Always be open to the possibility that things will be different!

Our teachers reside in the Upper World, and like our power animals, we may have one or two for a lifetime. There are others who remain with us for a shorter amount of time because they have something specific to teach us. Our teachers are usually human in form, and can be deities, saints, angels, heroes, or admired people who have passed away. Sometimes they are visible to us as we travel these realms, and other times they are invisible.

In most cases, our power animals lead us to the Upper World and stay with us as we explore the landscapes there. There are times, however, when I've found just myself in the Upper World talking to my teachers. Animals, too, may reside in the Upper World, and they serve as teachers rather than power allies, helping spirits, and companions.

Like the journey to the Lower World, the journey upward begins in an actual place in nature known to you. I use the same maple tree and I journey upward into the branches. Typically, the traveler will encounter a permeable barrier, such as a cloud or mist covering. After going through that barrier, you arrive in the Upper World. Sometimes these journeys can be surprising. On more than one occasion, I have traveled upward on an escalator. Several times I have found myself swimming through air to arrive in the Upper World, coming out of a fountain.

Usually, your teachers will be there and will greet you immediately. They are eager to teach you. My primary teacher is the woman I previously described who has three phases. There is also the man I described who transforms into different races and lives in a pavilion-type building, who I usually encounter in the library of that building, surrounded by books and the most up-to-date-technology.

Upper World Journey Basics

- Pick an actual place in nature that goes upward that you know well.

- Ask your power animals to assist you.

- State your intention clearly three times: "I am going to the Upper World to meet my teacher."

- Journey upward, meet your teacher, and talk with them.

- When the signal to return is sounded, follow the same path-way back to the starting point.

When you return to this world of consciousness, take the time to write down your experience. Think about ways you can connect with your teacher on this plane of existence. If you are journeying in a group, talk about the journey. Be ready for magic to happen. You are likely to find that the lessons they teach you continue in this plane of existence. Amazing synchronicities and coincidences will occur. If your teachers give you a chore to carry out, it is appropriate to find appropriate ways to continue the lesson in your everyday life. That is the work of the shaman—to take the wisdom of the other worlds and make it applicable and real in this world.

You will probably find that your relationship with your teacher is a little more formal than your relationships with your power animals. That does not mean it isn't an affectionate and fun-loving relationship, but your teachers have different missions than your power animals. Sometimes these differences are subtle and nuanced, but there is generally a greater sense of respect and perhaps a little more distance with your teachers. I think it is because of the relationship between teacher and student, where the teacher possesses greater wisdom and knowledge. That does not mean you can't have a good time, and even some fun, but the relationship is more instructive than sociable. In my experiences, our teachers are motivated by love and respect, and our relationship with them is deep and wonderful.

Journey Five:
Journey to the Middle World

My intention was to meet the Ancient Mother of Water. The drumbeat started and I sank into the trance. There was rain and water everywhere. The ground was soaked and moisture dripped off the leaves of the trees. 'Well, it has been a very wet summer,' I thought. I found myself in a cave, where rivulets of water made tinkly music as a background. Emerging from the darkness was a woman who was clothed in a dark cape. She spoke to me of many things as we walked along. We came to a big underground pool that looked just like a poolside at a very fancy hotel. She threw back the hood of her cloak and I could see a head of short silver hair. She had eyes the color of the sea in the sunlight—they sparkled with glee. She threw off her cloak and stood before me in a turquoise bathing suit—very fancy with lots of embellishments. She put her hands on her hips, walked to the side of the pool, and dove in. She was joined by several women, and they swam and danced in the pool. And then she reached up and pulled me in. I swam . . .

The Middle World journeys are in this plane of existence, and usually in the present, though the experiences and possibilities are without limit. Our Middle World guides are our power animals and spirit guides, though sometimes, in my experience, the fey creatures of the Middle World also serve as our guides. We may also find that the higher selves of people and animal companions still living will reach out and help us on our journeys through this world. We journey to places in the Middle World for information that helps us cope with our daily lives, for wisdom in our spiritual lives, and to seek out the creatures of the realms hidden to the physical eyes. The elemental spirits, the faery folk, devas, and other creatures may speak to us on these journeys.

Another task that can be done in the Middle World is to help ailing and dead spirits of people on this plane. People who are unable to understand their illnesses may have their higher selves talk to us and give us guidance. People who have died and not yet found their way to the next level of existence may need our help. This is particularly true of people who have died suddenly. Often, people journey to the spirit of the land where they live, or a land where there is much conflict, in order to understand the events that happen in ordinary time and space. Intense healing work, such as extractions or soul retrievals, is also done in the Middle World.

The landscape of the Middle World will look very much like the landscape of this world. There will be differences in texture, nuance, lighting, and view because time no longer exists and the hidden realms are likely to be revealed. When we return from these journeys, our understanding of our own world is transformed as the sacred reveals itself to us. We gain a deeper understanding of the mystery and magick that surrounds us.

Middle World Journey Basics

* Choose a place that exists in nature; be as specific as possible in your visualization.

* Ask your power animals to help you and state your intention three times: "I am going to my favorite place (name it) to find a story or song of the place."

* As the drumbeat starts, call your power animals to help you with your intention.

* Journey to your special place with your power animals and ask your question.

* Listen, look, and observe.

* When the signal to return is given, return by the same pathway.

When you return from this journey, write, draw, sing, or record your experiences. Find ways to share the story or song you found with others; you can create a collage, draw a picture, or write a poem. You don't even have to say that you got this inspiration in trance; you can just show your commemoration to others.

These five journeys are the basic journeys for the modern shamanic practitioner. If you practice, practice, practice, you will become adept at walking between the worlds. You will be a shamanic practitioner. To become strong and wise in the ways of the trance, you must walk between the worlds, record the wisdom of those journeys, and then apply the knowledge that you have gained. If you regularly journey and find wisdom that you apply to your life, you will find that power and grace become a part of your life and your being.

Most importantly, you will experience the interconnectedness of all life. You will find that you have an important vital place in the web of life, and that others in that web are happy and grateful for your presence there. You will find that even as a single human being, you are never alone and never without aid, solace, and laughter. You will experience the universal life force in all the beings that you encounter, and they will experience that same vital force in you. In your body, mind, spirit, and emotions, you will know that you matter, and that others matter too. The heartbeat of the Universe beats in your being.

Practice, Practice, Practice
Some Suggestions for Further Journeywork

By now, you have realized that in order to become a shamanic practitioner, you must journey. There are extraordinary times; times of great crises, in which, in addition to your other spiritual work, you can journey to the other realms to seek succor, support, and wisdom. In ordinary times, as part of your training and education in esoteric work, you can do journeys to seek information or to build your skills. In my regular journey group, participants often run out of ideas because they don't have (thank Heavens) a big predicament in their life at the present time. It is useful to have a list of journeys that you can take that will help you gain wisdom and skill, but aren't done under the shadow of calamity. Journeying can bring you practical solutions to your real-world problems, as well as spiritual growth. This kind of work makes a very good augmentation to health issues, but is no substitute for medical care.

The following are suggestions for further journeying, and you can modify them, use them as springboards for other ideas, or reject them completely! These suggestions are free-form ideas, and you will need to construct strong intentions from them when you journey. While I've suggested things for Lower, Upper, and Middle Worlds, your perspective may be different, and in those cases you should go with your instincts, for you are correct.

On another note, there are many, many more journeys that help build skills as a shamanic practitioner. There are journeys to take within the body for healing, journeys to help the souls of the departed journey to the land of Death, and journeys to mend the soul, just to name a few. These are the journeys of an experienced practitioner and are considered advanced work, so they are not covered here. Stay focused on your practice and learn all you can. Sometimes those kinds of journeys happen spontaneously, when Spirit decides you are ready, and other times, you will know when it is time to seek out further instruction.

Lower World Journeys

- Journey on issues of health and health care. Be specific; for example, journey on your knee pain, or something similar. I did a series of journeys to explore each of my chakras.

- Journey on creative projects and ask for energy, ideas, and inspiration.

- Journey on issues surrounding food, nutrition, and exercise.

- Journey to test your gut reactions to issues in your life.

- Journey on work-related issues, particularly those that involve emotional issues with co-workers, clients, and supervisors.

- Journey on money, bills, and other practical aspects of life.

- Journey on family, children, and friends. Again, be specific in your intention, such as "How can I help my daughter with her struggles with social studies?"

- Journey for power animals when you start something new. For example, if you are beginning to study Tarot, ask for a power animal to assist you with that study.

- Journey to the spirit of specific (natural) things, like a crystal or an herb.

- Journey to the spirit of specific manufactured or human-created things, such as your house or your car.

Upper World Journeys

- Journey to your teachers when you start a new creative project and ask for inspiration, insights, and intuition.

- Journey for wisdom concerning intellectual endeavors, help on tests, and schoolwork.

- Journey to your teachers for guidance when beginning (or in the midst of) a new course of study.

- Journey to meet a new deity or spirit with whom you are working.

- Journey to your teachers for guidance when big issues come up in your life.

- Journey on issues about work, especially those concerns about projects, new endeavors, and writing. I find the Upper World teachers particularly helpful when I have a presentation or a meeting where I need to pitch an idea or defend a budget request.

- Journey to the Upper World when you feel everything is going well, but you feel a little restless, uneasy, or bored. Ask your teachers for the wisdom of this time, or ask them for a new project, although that could indeed be one of those cases of "Be careful what you ask for!"

- Journey to the Upper World during those times when you feel stalled and unsure which way to go next.

- Journey to the Upper World during those times when you have to make a choice, when you are at the crossroads, or when you are being asked to choose "the lesser of two evils."

- Journey to the Upper World when you feel your ethics are being challenged, and ask for wisdom and guidance.

- When you are entering a new phase of life, such as graduation from college, journey to your teachers for advice on the next steps in your journey.

Middle World Journeys

- Journey to the spirit of the land where you live, and ask how you can live in harmony with the land. What does it need most from you?

- Journey to the spirit of your house, apartment, or dwelling to gain insight or information. This is especially helpful if you need to do repairs or are contemplating a renovation. If you regard your dwelling as sacred space, working in harmony with that space can give you some great ideas and save you some costly errors. "Should I replace my water heater?" might actually get you some information about your furnace!

- Journey to each of the directions to meet the guardians or spirits of that Direction.

- Journey to the elements and the spirits and creatures of those elements.

- Journey to the spirit of your drum and or rattle after you have done the exercises in the previous sections, and after you have worked regularly with your drum and rattle for awhile.

- Journey on questions about your plants, gardens, and other outdoor activities.

- Journey to the spirits of specific items, such as rocks and crystals; to specific breeds of plants and trees; and to breeds of animals, birds, amphibians, and other creatures.

- Journey to the spirit of a body of water near you. It can be an ocean, a lake, a stream, or a creek.

- Journey to the spirit of landmarks, especially those close to where you live. These could be waterfalls, gorges, mountains, forests, swamps, even whole areas and islands.

The journeys you choose will bring you more information to walk this path and bless your life in the everyday world. Your daily life and your spiritual life will become more pleasantly blended as you seek the wisdom of other realms. By the same token, you should not substitute journeywork and magical work for the wisdom of the everyday world. By all means, go to the doctor, call the plumber, and pay your insurance! Spirit calls us to live authentically in all the worlds that we walk. Inside the rhythm of the drum, you can find many insights and inspirations. Illusions will fall away as you discover the treasure hidden around you. You, your life, and your spiritual path will become more genuine and real to you as you practice. In the practice, you become. Becoming is a continuous act, and you will never stop as long as your heart beats and your spirit soars. You learn every step and dance every step as you follow the path of the shamanic practitioner. May your practice be blessed with joy!

Power Objects: The Tool Kit of the Shamanic Practitioner

The drumbeat took me quickly, and I was in the Underworld tunnel. Instead of walking, I was in a boat with Polar Bear behind me. We were riding a swiftly flowing stream of water, like those rides in the water park. Polar Bear was having a whole lot of fun! Because I was in the front, I was being splashed by the water more often. It was refreshing and exhilarating. Finally, we stopped and the scene transformed into a place at the edge of the woods. We were in front of a very humble home, with gardens and animals all around us. To the side, there was a small yard with an herb garden planted in a spiral. In the center of the spiral was a cauldron over a fire pit. The fire was built and going strong; there were glowing embers in the pit.

A woman of an indeterminate age came out of the house, and she beckoned to me to follow her. We walked the spiral inward. Her skirts brushed the herbs, and I could smell mint, thyme, and other herbs I did not recognize. We approached the cauldron, and she began to stir the pot. She went to the garden, selected some herbs, and put them in the pot. She set some of her pickings aside. She began to hum a song, and I recognized it as my power song, so I sang it along with her. This went on for a long time.

Finally the concoction was done, and she put a little bit of it in a goblet and told me to drink it. I did, and it was vile. But I felt much better. She took the herbs that she had set aside, and held them in her hand. "Smell," she said, and I sniffed them. "Mint," I said. "Yes," she replied. "Whenever you need clarity, go smell the mint."

If you know anyone who does shamanic work or incorporates shamanic work into their practices, you will have noticed that, in addition to their drums and rattles, they carry other objects, pouches, and bundles. These are the power objects of that person. Different traditions have different practices concerning these objects. Most importantly, the power objects of the practitioner are individual, and are tuned to the energy of the practitioner.

Power objects come to the practitioner in a variety of ways. In one way or another, the acquisition of a power object is guided through the shamanic journeywork of the person. For instance, the journey above tells you that mint is one of the herbs that assist me not only in my shamanic work, but also in my everyday life. I have a bed of mint in my front yard that grows rather wildly, but I routinely pick and breathe in its scent. It was given to me in a journey by one of my teachers. I don't carry the mint with me in a pouch, but it is readily available when I need it.

Often, the teachers, guides, and power animals of our journeys will give us objects to symbolize parts of our lives—for example, aspects that we need to strengthen. These objects are real and reside in nonordinary reality, and are part of our tool kit. We can actively use them when we are in meditation and trance state. We can visualize them in our meditations and trances, and continue to create a connection with these gifts of spirit.

More often than not, these tools will become solid and manifest themselves in ordinary reality. So many people have told me stories of designs, rings, stones, bracelets, and other things that have been given to them in their journeys, only to find them by coincidence at a craft fair or as a gift given by someone who has no idea what the object will mean to you, but says, "Here, I saw this and just had to get it for you." Know that this is not just random coincidence, but the spiritual realms reaching through the veil to give you the tools that you need.

In one journey, I was told to create a wand in this reality. I had a very graceful stick that came into my possession, though I cannot remember where it came from. I knew it was special, but I didn't know what to do with it, so I just kept it on an altar or in my cupboard of ritual items. In the journey, I was told what to do with it. I was to wrap it with multicolor embroidery thread and use it as part of my journeywork to understand the element of air. So in sacred space, I wrapped the stick with the thread, and then kept it on the altar while I did the air journeys. The wand itself did not appear in the journeys, but I have no doubt that it helped facilitate the wisdom I gained. Recently, I was given additional instructions on what to do with it. In this case, I lacked the skill to fulfill the instructions, but coincidentally, I found a workshop offered in just that skill. I took the class, and now I am ready to complete the task. This has been a long process, and the wisdom is slow in unveiling itself. Each time a new piece of the story is revealed, I am amazed at the interconnectedness of the various aspects of my life.

In the process of receiving and working with power objects, you will find that other skills are needed. Gardening, herbs, beading, leatherworking, painting, and other skills that engage your body are all practices that can express your inner visions. You will probably find that the urge to express the wisdom of your journeys will help you develop not only a practice of recording your journeys, but also other, more artistic practices. I quilt, do various kinds of needlework, and am interested in learning to bead. As your shamanic practice becomes integrated into your life, your outward expressions of this rich inner life will move into your exterior life.

Some onlookers may not know why your paintings are more powerful or reflect the magic of nature, but you will. Your dancing may take on a strength and beauty it has never had before. Or, you may break loose from your inhibitions and try something for which you felt you never had the talent. Your own special vision, talent, and abilities will become melded with your wisdom and power from the spiritual realms, and you will create beauty.

Activating and Attuning Power Objects

Often you will be given small stones, crystals, fetishes, herbs, and other objects in your journeys, and they will manifest almost immediately in this reality. You will either be instructed to carry these things with you, or you will want to have them close to your body. Practitioners make pouches that they wear around their necks or carry in their pockets and purses. Some practitioners have pouches, bundles, and jewelry that they use only when they journey or do ceremony. They do this because the objects have been attuned to their personal energy. This attunement is done in a variety of ways, depending on the traditions of the practitioner. The most important thing to remember about the power of attunement is to actively use the object and maintain your connection with it. If you gain an object and keep it on the top shelf of your closet in an old shoebox, the power will dissipate and disappear. The power of these objects is not inherent, but is the result of honorable use.

Ceremony for Creating and
Attuning a Power Object

In recent months, I have gone to a couple of sacred crafts workshops where there have been two objectives; one is to create the object, and the second is to cleanse and consecrate the object to spiritual use. In both cases, because of the skill level of the students, the second objective was submerged into the first of learning the skill to create the object. Because people did not have the skill to begin with, they needed extra time to learn it. Consequently, the cleansing and consecrating portion of the workshop did not take place. So a gentle word of advice—take the time to learn the craft beforehand, just enough to create the object you wish to have as a power object, and then learn to consecrate it!

You may also wish to divide this ceremony into two parts. In the first, you create the object, and in the second, you consecrate it to your use. In the space between the two parts, place your object on an altar; or, if you don't have one permanently set up, in a place that is safe, cleansed, and sacred. If you do the ceremony in two parts, you are actually doing two ceremonies, so you will do the preparation, spirit calls, and farewells twice. Whatever you do, be sure to enjoy the process, and be open to the blessings of Spirit.

Tools Needed: Drum, rattle, and incense or smudge stick. The tools and items needed to create your object.

Optional: Soothing music, recorded chants, or other appropriate background sounds.

To Prepare: Prepare your space and altar, and gather items for comfort. If you think this will take a large amount of time, have blessed water, juice, and food available; be sure to attend to your comforts. Become ready by grounding and connecting to the earth. Actively visualize putting away your anxieties and distractions. Cleanse distracting energies away from the space by smudging or rattling around the space, paying attention to the assembled items.

Call in the Spirits and Creatures of the Directions; Call in the Deities: Call in the spirits and creatures that guide you. Below are some suggested words, and be sure to call in the teachers, allies, and power animals that have assisted you along the way. If there are specific deities with which you work, call them in as well.

Spirits and creatures of the East, messengers of inspiration: Fly to me from the dawning of wisdom and bring with you clarity, discernment, and vitality. Inspire me with the freshness of spring, and rouse my mind with ideas and thoughts. Hail and welcome!

Spirits and creatures of the South, keepers of passionate will: Spark my spirit with resolve and persistence, and in the strong sunlight of the noonday sun, bring me strength, endurance, and determination. Invigorate me with the fire of summer, and rouse my determination to achievement. Hail and welcome!

Spirits and creatures of the West, keepers of the dreaming heart: Soothe and cleanse my spirit with your mysteries and magic, and at the beauty of the setting sun, bring me compassion, love, and pleasure. Inspire my feelings with new depths and healing, and rouse my heart with kindness and beauty. Hail and welcome!

Spirits and creatures of the North, keepers of silent strength: Ground and center my spirit with your stability, darkness, and enchantment;

and in the deepest night, bring me understanding, wisdom, and revelation. Inspire my soul with surprise and perception. Hail and welcome!

Spirits and creatures of Below, keepers of earthy wisdom: Root my spirit with your healing, purifying strength, and in the place of no place, bring me connection. Inspire me with the love of the Earth Mother. Hail and welcome!

Spirits and creatures of Above, keepers of celestial wisdom: Lift my spirit with your illuminating light and infinite wisdom, and in this time of not time, bring me wholeness. Inspire me with the wisdom of the heavens. Hail and welcome!

Great Creators, Gods and Goddesses of the realms of Spirit and of this earth: Join me in my sacred work. Bring your healing, blessings, power, and grace, and through the limitlessness of all the worlds, bless my work with your understanding, love, and peace. Hail and welcome!

Focus Your Intention: State here that you are going to create your power object, and then consecrate its use. As you work, try to keep your attention focused on the work you are doing and the purpose of the finished object. Let extraneous thoughts about tonight's supper, the phone bill, or an argument with a neighbor move out of your thoughts. Keep your focus on your intention as you build the energy into the object.

Create the Object: As your hands work, sing songs and say prayers. Give thanks to the spirits that guided you do to this work. If you are playing soothing or sacred music, hum along or sing the chants. If you have a power song, sing it as you create this object.

When It Is Finished: Make a final flourishing statement such as, "Spirits and creatures of all the directions, teachers, spirits, allies, the divine beings of light and dark, bless this work. May it always be powerful, and may I always use it for the greater good." Take the object to your altar, and smudge it with healing herbs so that any possible negativity is cleared.

Attune to the Power Object

Stand in the center of your space, holding your object near your heart. Take a deep breath and feel your energy fill your body, from head to toe and to the tips of your fingers. Feel your energy move into the object, filling it with beauty and light. Take one long, deep breath and feel the object connect with you. Breathe your energy into the object.

Continue breathing in this manner, and cast your awareness down to your feet and send roots down into the earth. As your roots go downward, feel the energy of the Earth Mother meld into the roots. Find a place to loop your roots, down deep in the earth, and stabilize yourself there, firmly but flexibly. Through your roots, breathe up the energy of the Earth Mother into yourself and feel it meld and dance with the energy inside you. When you are filled with the energy of the Earth Mother, cast your awareness to the object in your hands, and breathe this melded energy into the object. Continue to breathe this combined energy into the object.

Continue breathing in this manner, and then cast your awareness to the crown of your head. Send your energy outward into the Universe, and feel the energy of the Universe reach out to you and embrace you. As you are embraced, feel this energy merge with the combined energy of you and the Earth Mother. Feel it move downward through your crown and into your body. Breathe in that energy and feel it meld together, a triplicity of beauty and delight. When that energy has filled you from head to toe and to the tips of your fingers, cast your awareness to your hands and the object there.

Breathe energy into that object. Keep breathing deeply so that you are connected to the object, and it is filled with the combined energy. When the connection is deep and strong, gently move your roots away from the anchoring spot and bring them gently back to your feet. Then cast your awareness up into the Universe where you are held in that embrace, and gently move out of that embrace. Move the energy back into yourself. Stay connected to your object, and breathe deeply once so that your awareness is completely back into your space. Breathe again to fully open your eyes and awareness to your space.

With your object in hand, move clockwise around the circle, and present your object to the Direction. Ask for blessings and honor as you move. Go East, South, West, North, Below, and Above. Offer the object to any deities that you have called in. When you are done, place the object on your altar and say a prayer of thanksgiving. It is done!

Farewell to the Spirits and Creatures
of the Directions, to the Deities

Creatures and spirits of the North, keepers of the final silence: Thank you for your presence here at this ceremony, and thank you for the blessings you have bestowed. Go with my thanks and my blessings. Hail and farewell!

Creatures and spirits of the West, keepers of the dreams and mysteries: Thank you for your presence here at this ceremony, and thank you for the blessings you have bestowed. Go with my thanks and my blessings. Hail and farewell!

Creatures and spirits of the South, keepers of flaming passion: Thank you for your presence here at this ceremony, and thank you for the blessings you have bestowed. Go with my thanks and my blessings. Hail and farewell!

Creatures and spirits of the East, messengers of intuition: Thank you for your presence here at this ceremony, and thank you for the blessings you have bestowed. Go with my thanks and my blessings. Hail and farewell!

Creatures and spirits of Below, keepers of the earth energy: Thank you for your presence here at this ceremony, and thank you for the blessings you have bestowed. Go with my thanks and my blessings. Hail and farewell!

Creatures and spirits of Above, keepers of the celestial wisdom: Thank you for your presence here at this ceremony, and thank you for the blessings you have bestowed. Go with my thanks and my blessings. Hail and farewell!

Your ceremony is finished and your object is consecrated and attuned to your energy. Store it in a safe and sacred place when you are not using it. You will need to continue to attune yourself to the object by using it in your journeywork, ceremonies, and meditations. You may want to do the contemplation exercises that you did with your drum and rattle. Your object has a voice, and you will want to listen to what it has to say to you.

Power Songs and Dances
The Power of Song

I hadn't been doing shamanic journeywork for very long. Our group came together in a dark room, lit only by a couple of candles. We sat on the floor and we drummed together for several minutes. For all I know it could have been days, so timeless was the drumming. Suddenly, someone began to sing. I'm not sure if there were words; I couldn't hear the tune. All I knew was that someone gave voice to their experiences. Another person began to sing. I stopped listening as the drum took me to another realm. When the drumming stopped, the facilitator said, "Tonight you will journey to find your power song."

I settled myself in the dark, covered my eyes, and stated my intention three times, along with a desperate little prayer that this would really work. I was not confident. The drumming took me to my place in nature and I went quickly down the tunnel, and ended up at the farm, in a time when my grandfather was still working the land. I was a child, and as was usual in those days, I was following him around, watching him and "helping him." I walked behind him as he fed Bob, the horse. I gave Bob a corncob and felt his soft nuzzle brush mine. I watched Granddad go up to the loft and send hay down to Bob. I followed him as he fed Peanuts, the pig. We both fed the chickens. I realized that I was hearing him hum what I always thought of as his "tuneless tune." He always hummed as he worked. I started to hum the song too. Suddenly, I was in a circle in the middle of a wood, surrounded by my power animals, as well as my gardening female teacher. She was humming the tuneless tune with some extra notes added at the end. All the animals began to sing this song. Then it was my turn, and I started to sing as well. Granddad's tuneless tune with my notes added at the end. My soul song, my power song, connected me with love to my past, to my family, and to my spiritual life.

The shamanic practitioner has a magical tool kit full of tangible and intangible objects. The essence of shamanic practice is to create change in either yourself or others, using energy and information gained by walking in other realms. One of the most potent and powerful tools for the practitioner is song. Adding your own voice to the process of journeywork and ceremony has great power. Singing and humming your song creates vibrations within your body, and this vibrating energy attracts and causes the vibrations of the Universe to move into your harmony. As I've said, this process of harmonizing energies is called entrainment, and you've seen it happen as you move into harmony with the drumbeat.

You will have many songs as you develop a regular shamanic practice, and you will have one that speaks to your soul and sings forth from that very center of your being. It will be one that will sing of your power, your joy, and your experiences of life. It may have words, but it may not, as mine does not. Your power song will give you power when you have none, will remind you of your connection to all of life when you are lonely, and will comfort you when you need it. You will find that it comes spontaneously from you at times—those are times to examine, to find out why your power song has unexpectedly surfaced. You will find your power song to be a resource when you need a solution.

Sometimes, shamanic practitioners find their power song immediately, and sometimes it can take a long time to discover it. Singing, voice, and judgments about talent all come into play. I thought it was astonishing that I found mine right away, since I didn't like to sing in front of people. What helped me get over that is the loud drumming, which makes it hard for people to hear you. The drumming is also carrying people away into their own journeys, so they are not really listening to the singing. Having a power song has gone a long way in helping me overcome my shyness about singing in public—I don't sing well, but I can sing loud!

Power songs are an important and essential tool for those who walk between the worlds. Songs are used in healing both the body and the soul. When working with others, the shamanic practitioner must use their voice to teach, lead, and heal. So, the first healing that needs to be done is to heal any self-doubt about your own effectiveness as someone who walks between the worlds. Finding your song and singing it is one of those simple steps that is a big leap.

Many of my students have had a lot to overcome when seeking their power songs. Shyness, self-criticism, and doubt are just a few inhibitions that keep students from finding their strengths. Spirits will ask that we address those issues, and the power song may be the way they are addressed. In addition to the journey to find the power song, I have developed a guided visualization to help people seek their song. As you do the meditation below, prepare your space and honor the meditation just as you would a shamanic journey. Ground and center yourself in this quiet space and begin.

Take a deep breath, and let it out fully. Take a deep breath, and let it out with a sigh. With that sigh, let out expectations. Take another deep breath. Hold it for a second, and let it out fully with a noise. Take another deep breath and let it out with a tone (ommmmm).

See yourself standing in your favorite place. It is night, and the dark is beautiful. Listen to the sounds around you, and drink in the deep satisfying happiness of being in your favorite place. Know that you are completely safe as you listen to the sounds, smell the aromas, and look into the night. Look to the horizon and see that the moon has risen, full and beautiful. See the beautiful light fill the sky. Feel the beauty and the peace of the moon as it rises above you. Breathe in the beauty of the night as you stand there, centered.

As you watch the moon, see her shape become that of a woman, the Goddess. As she takes shape, see her come down to the earth some distance away from you. Begin to walk toward her, taking in the sight of her. She begins to walk toward you, and she is singing a song. Hear the song and let its beauty fill you. Feel the vibrations of the song fill you, and feel your body begin to hum with the song. This is the song of your soul. She begins to sing the notes and you sing along with her. The tones are perfect for you, and fill your heart, body, and soul. Sing along with her as you both sing your soul. Perfect and beautiful, the notes fill you. If there are words, hear the words with your ears and your heart. Remember.

She sings to you as she approaches you. She holds you in her embrace, the Mother Goddess. Look deep into her eyes and see yourself reflected there. She gives you a word from your song that is your word for this journey at this time. Remember the word and say it to yourself as a talisman for as long as you need it.

She sits with you. Talk with her, and ask her what is in your heart. When it is time, you will find a gift in your pocket, around you or in *your hand. Give it to her with a word of thanks. She will give you a final hug and a gift. Take it, and walk back to where you were in your favorite place. Watch the moon set and the dawn begin. Breathe deeply, and come back to your space.*

Many of my students do this meditation several times, and then go on a journey to find their song. They find that it does help them.

Sometimes the song shows up when we least expect it, or when our intention is to journey for something else. For example, a practitioner may be seeking information about a new job or assistance with an interview and find their power song. Never underestimate the power of serendipity!

Journey to Find your Power Song

- Go to your place in nature.

- State your intention three times: I ask my power animal to take me on a journey to find my power song.

- As the drumming begins, ask your power animal to come to you and ask it to help you find your power song.

- Journey!

Spend some time drumming and singing your song. Make sure that it is part of your blood and bones. After that, when you hear the drumbeat, you will sing your song regardless of any other inhibitions your might feel!

You will find that other songs will come to you as well. One time, while driving the highway between Baltimore and my home in upstate New York, I had the impulse to turn off the radio. A song came to me. I sang it for miles and miles and miles in that driving trance that happens when you go the same speed over familiar roads. Along with the song came words and a poem. It was my wish to give the poem to my students to have as they move from one path to another, and when they cross the threshold into a new initiation. You will find that poem, "All the Empty Places" at the beginning of this book.

The Power of Dance

It was a difficult time of life for me. Death had rampaged into my life when the man with whom I had an extremely difficult relationship died suddenly, a young man. I was left with the aftermath—grief, mourning, and dealing with the reactions of others. I found out about lies he had told me, so there was much anger. More damaging was the resentment. Resentment of the work I had to do to clean up what he had left behind, resentment of the emotions of others that were inflicted upon me. I was stressed, sleep-disturbed, and twitchy in a variety of ways. I hadn't been to shamanic drumming for a long time, but I finally made myself go.

The facilitator told us we were to do a letting go ceremony, and we were to journey to where we needed to let go. I knew immediately that I had to let go of resentment. The drumming started, and the journey was awful. I went from one situation to another in which I was resentful, pouty, and angry. It was horrible, and it went on forever. I went deep into my resentment.

The drum called us back, and we were given a piece of paper to write down our issues to let go. "RESENTMENT," I wrote in big, bold letters. As everyone drummed, one by one we put our papers into the fire. I watched my resentment burst into flames and disappear.

Then, we were told to dance. My worst nightmare—dancing! As the facilitator explained, we retain memories of our emotions in our body; in our tissues, bones, and sinew. Lingering there, those emotions cause great damage on all kinds of levels. She told us that to get rid of those emotions, we need to dance, and as we dance, see those things we let go leave our body and transform into bright energy. She put on a tape of many drums with an incredible drumbeat that seemed to get me. I forgot my self-consciousness and just danced. At times I just jumped up and down to the beat. I shook my hands and it seemed like energy came out of my fingers and changed into green sparks of light. On and on I danced. Getting lighter and lighter. Energy rolled off me and I could see whirling light surround me. It was powerful.

We came back to circle, and as I sat down, I realized that I had stopped clenching my jaw. I wasn't shutting in my resentment, and I couldn't get that feeling back. It was gone, eradicated from me by the drum, the fire, and the dance.

Movement empowers us in ways that no other method can. It moves us beyond the "can'ts" of our conscious mind, into the realm of the wordless. The journey described above is one of the most powerful I have ever experienced, and it is because of the dance. Most traditions practice some kind of sympathetic magical banishing through fire, and I had done that many times. This was more profoundly transforming because I banished resentment from my thinking, from my emotions, and from my body. It was an amazing experience. Dance does that, and when the damaging emotions are cleared away, you are filled with healing energy.

When your song fills you, and the Universe moves into your harmony, you will find the urge to dance. The drum will call you to dance, and all your songs will also call you to dance. Dance is another powerful tool for the shamanic practitioner. You have already danced your power animal, and will find other ways to dance as well. Much of the work of shamanic healers involves movement and dancing. When the need to dance fills you and the urge to dance calls you, heed the call and dance every dance.

Giving Thanks and the Energy of Connection

Infused throughout shamanic practice and all spiritual practices is thanksgiving, to thank those who help us for their guidance, assistance, and blessings. While we may not understand the motives and needs of creatures and spirits of other realms, we do perceive their generosity and sometimes sacrifice as they help us grow and become spiritual beings. To thank them is a way of honoring their work with us. Sometimes when the revelations about ourselves are difficult, it is hard to remember to be thankful. I have even made my thanksgiving statements in a tone of irony, but I do thank them and I mean it on some level, even if it is rueful.

Because these beings live in different realms and have very different abilities and powers, we often think of them as superior beings, and perhaps they are. I do know that they are beings that are in need of our blessings as well. Whatever gifts we can give them are a blessing to them; that is why I include "go with our thanks and our blessings" in my farewells. I don't understand why the spirits would need my blessings, but they do. I am honored and delighted that I can give them something they need and want, and that it is within my power to do so.

Thanksgiving puts us in the flow of the Universe, the movement of energy, blessings, and love that occurs all around us. By giving thanks, we are able to hear the harmony of the Universe more truly in our hearts and souls. You may find that the practice of thanksgiving removes blockages you may have surrounding money and power. Cravings, stinginess, and impotence may fade away, or you may find yourself actively working on those issues in your life, and that those seemingly insurmountable issues grow fainter and eventually disappear.

The active practice of blessings and thanksgiving will seem self-conscious at first, but with persistence you will find that it is second nature. I believe that our natural wholeness is meant for harmony, generosity, and thankfulness. As we consciously move ourselves in that direction of wholeness, we move with the natural flow of the Universe, and blockages begin to dissolve and then disappear.

When those blockages and barriers disappear, we find ourselves more aware of the interconnectedness of life. Our understanding of relationships becomes richer, more textural, and more beautiful. It helps us get through the hard times to have the knowledge that beneath our sorrow and grief is a realm that supports and shares with us. As we deepen our connection with an abundant and loving Universe, we find our connections to other people also become more nuanced. None of us are exempt from pain, sorrow, and grief, but we are also entitled to love, grace, and power. We experience it when we stop resisting the energy of All-That-Is, and move into the loving arms of the Universe. Dark and light, sweet and bitter, evil and good become melded into blessings for all.

Merging with the Universe:
The Dance of Ecstasy

The drum started to beat its rhythm and my heart began to keep time with the drum. I could feel the beat moving me deeper into trance. I was in a cave, rich and wet. The cave walls glistened with water drops, and everything had a rich, lush burgundy color. The cave floor was moist and springy with the dampness. Suddenly I realized I was in my own womb. An old woman dressed in a long, hooded cloak came out of the shadows and I recognized her as the Ancient Mother of Water. She told me to forget my worries and live in joy. Suddenly we were by a large, beautiful pool. She threw back the hood of her cloak and shook out her hair. It was gray and springy, and still a glorious head of hair.

She looked at me and grinned. We looked at the pool and several women popped up from the water, all with gray hair. They each raised one hand. The Ancient Mother threw off her cloak; she was dressed in a one-piece bathing suit, the kind they design for older women to disguise their so-called figure problems. She struck a pose with her hands on her hips and her chin up; looking to all the world like a super-hero. She dove into the water, and she and the other women treated me to a fabulous water ballet. Their exuberance and delight in the water and the dance was contagious.

I ran to the edge of the pool, drawn by their feelings, their splashing, and their pleasure. Polar Bear nudged me from behind, in the small of my back. I dove in, and the water embraced me. I could feel the happiness of the swimmers surround me like electricity conducted through water. I was electrified and overjoyed. I let the happiness fill me and I danced in the water. Hands joined with mine as I danced.

I merged with the water until I was part of this throbbing, beautiful dance of water, contagious glee, and magical togetherness.

It is hard to describe the state of ecstasy in prose. Ecstasy is a poetic experience that moves our conscious thinking mind into a place where there is no thought, no criticism, no self-consciousness, no analysis, and no sense of time pressure. Ecstasy moves into the world of feeling, pictures, and symbols, and when we embrace that place and merge into its flowing love, we are the ecstasy.

The word "ecstasy" comes from the Greek word *ekstasis*, which means the withdrawal of the soul from the body in mystic or visionary trance. Phrases like, "I took leave of my senses," and "I was beside myself," are echoes of an ecstatic state. The word in classical times was linked to insanity and frenzy, indicating a distrust in uncontrolled, rapturous states. This moving outside of our egocentric selves helps us to move more freely among the spirits who reach out to us. We are free, unfettered, and open. Having willingly surrendered our temporally bound ego, we move joyfully and willingly into the embrace of the Universe.

This feeling of ecstasy connects us to all creatures and beings in all the realms. It moves us from a state of separateness and aloneness to a state of interconnected bliss. We know who we are, assuredly, but we also know that we are more than our bodies and our accomplishments. We are part of the whole; we are part of the Universe.

Time and place lose their meaning for us when we find ecstasy. Think of a hobby, an activity, a place, or a feeling where you forgot yourself, forgot what time it was, forgot where you were—a time when you were completely concentrated and absorbed. A time when you felt somehow connected to something greater than yourself, even when you didn't know what it was. These are all moments that can be considered ecstatic.

There are parts of my personal story, the one I tell when I speak of how I found the Goddess, that I now know as ecstatic moments. During one of those striking moments, it was like the Heavens opened up and all of the stars reached out and held me in their embrace. Even though I knew I was sitting on the hood of our family station wagon, I also knew that I was in a place where all the worries I had fell away. It was a place where everything felt still and full. Full of what, I'm not certain, since I was just a kid. At the time, I didn't care; I just felt the feeling. I breathed it in and felt it fill me. I could feel the darkness of the night sky even though it was the middle of the day. I could feel the stars twinkling with my heart rather than seeing them with my eyes. It was like they merged with me, and I could feel what it was like to be starlight in the darkness. And then, gently, the feeling receded, and I could hear my sister and brothers playing in the background. The sensation has never truly gone away, and I've had other similar experiences that remain in the fibers of my being as well.

Once we have had ecstatic moments, we retain them in our tissues and in our body, and we can call up those experiences and remember them. We can also create new ecstasies as we merge with the Universe. Doing what we love, regularly meditating in deep trance, dancing to the drum, and working with the Spirit in ritual are all part of our work as creatures of ecstasy.

As ecstasy merges with the Universe, we understand that all life on our planet and in our Universe breathes and throbs with consciousness. We understand it intellectually, but when we move in meditation, trance, and ritual, we understand it with our soul. We find that our barriers and boundaries change and become blended with the flow of the universal life energy. We move in harmony, and when we find that harmonious place, we sing the joy of our merging.

It is a beautiful place, this place of merging and emergence. We shift, we move, and we change within it. We find our heart, our bliss, and our joy. We find our tears, our laughter, and our sense of well-being. We infuse this feeling in nonordinary reality, and our everyday lives become vibrant and pulsating with life. Our chores and tasks become part of the magical life we are living. The experiences of ecstasy create a sense of understanding that centers us and grounds us in our emotions, spirit, and body. We appreciate more because we have experienced the appreciation of the Universe. We are loved, we are love, and we are loving. We heal and become whole, and in our wholeness we find our own divine holiness.

Even when we experience ecstasy with increasing frequency, it does not become familiar or commonplace. It is always an adventure, a joy rediscovered, and a connection that brings deeper bliss and understanding. Ecstasy should not have to be an unusual experience for us, something reserved for special occasions or not at all. It should be part of our treasured day, a gift of the spirit, and a gift from ourselves. If we are always connected, then we have the potential to be in the middle of our own wise ecstasy and delight.

Answering the Call of the Drum

The drumbeat begins and your heart begins to beat with the drum. You feel your heart begin to pump rhythm throughout your body.

Your blood attunes to the throbbing beat of the drum, and the beat fills your whole body. Your bones, tissues, cells, and skin begin to feel the beating of the drum. And you begin to dance. Your feet move with the beating of your heart, and your hands and arms are raised and move in concert with the harmony coming from the drum and from within. Your mind flows into the rhythm and your soul dances each movement. You are the drumbeat, you are the harmony, and you are the rhythm.

As you develop a regular schedule of journeys and your shamanic trance meditations grow, you will feel the pull of the drum, the heartbeat of the Universe. You will find that you will move naturally into the harmony of the Universe. You will feel the interconnectedness of life, and know that you are not alone.

In traditional cultures, the call to be a shaman happens in a couple of ways; either through an inherited family role, or through a crisis that is really a call to change. Even in cultures where the role of the shaman is a family one, the call comes in the form of a crisis. The crisis is usually some kind of illness that forces the individual to move outside of their comfort zone and into the world of Spirit to seek answers and find solutions. Part of the work is to find the power to overcome the illness or other crisis.

Once the crisis is overcome, the shaman is changed forever, and cannot go back to the life they had before. But the shaman, now changed, does return to community to find that there is a new role and a new challenge for the shaman to take on. This challenge is to continue to build the power already gained to create more change. In traditional cultures, the work of the shaman was done in service to the community. The individual lived deeply connected to the community, and all changes in individuals created changes in the community.

In our modern culture, the connectedness of community is fractured and often unrecognizable. The call of the drum for the modern practitioner is also often found in a crisis. More often than not, the crisis is an illness of the soul that creates a need for a greater awareness of the soul. The call to work shamanically for the modern person is also a call to use the power gained to create change. Often the first and sometimes only place where change can take place is within the individual. This is not selfishness.

My first shamanic teacher, SunRaven, often said that, "the first duty of the healer is to heal Self." Without healing the self, the healer cannot understand the struggles of others. Moreover, our connectedness to each other and the worlds around us, while fractured, has not disappeared. Often, our first chore is to rebuild and recreate the interconnectedness of life around us. This can include rebuilding and healing relationships, greater spiritual understanding, working in the community, or bodily healing.

Those who already practice a spiritual path including the earth-based religions such as Wicca and Witchcraft will find a call to meld their practices. Rather than doing both separately, to mirror the interconnectedness of all life, wiccans and witches are finding ways to connect their shamanic practice with the spiritual path of the Goddess and the God.

CHAPTER 4

THE REALMS OF THE WITCH: ENTWINING THE ECSTASIES OF THE SHAMAN AND THE WITCH

We are a circle
Within a circle
With no beginning
And never ending.

This pagan chant sings an important message to us because it tells us that we are all connected, interconnected, and part of the web of life, and that the energy of the Universe sings within us. This interconnectedness of life and the knowledge that everything has life force energy within is also the teaching of the shamanic practitioner. This, too, is the message of Wicca and Witchcraft; that we move in harmony with the energies of the Goddess and the God, dancing with all others who hear the same heartbeat. In both practices, it is the ecstatic experience and our direct interaction with the sacred that calls to us to walk this path. Each one of us is in direct contact with the realms of Spirit and with the Divine, and when we answer the call we move beyond ourselves into ecstasy.

My spiritual journey into Wicca and Witchcraft came at the same time as my explorations into shamanic journeywork. To me, both things have always been inextricably linked, and I consciously seek to meld these practices into one. It is not always easy to do, because many shamanic teachers are not wiccan, and many wiccan teachers are not shamanic practitioners. Often those who practice both Wicca and Shamanism do not teach both together. Truthfully, classes in these two practices pull from different audiences, and many students are interested in one or the other, but not both. In fairness, these subjects are so different that, for many people, to learn both at the same time would send them into information and sensory overload. The experiences gained through the teachings, coupled with learning new ways of seeing and thinking, would be overwhelming.

It is natural to learn Wicca and Shamanism as separate paths, but they are so closely linked in concept and feeling that each practice calls to be entwined with the other. These two practices teach us that there is no separateness and demand that they be practiced together; the challenge is to integrate them. In many ways, the integration happens naturally, slowly, and with a change of consciousness. As students new to Wicca, our worldview changes and expands. We find the sacred everywhere, not just in church. When we begin to see the Divine in everything around us, the world opens new doors to us, and we see with new eyes. We find the heartbeat of the Universe wherever we look. Magic appears to us, shimmering in the summer heat, and blowing into our lives on the cold winter winds. The autumn leaves tell us the story of nature and God; God sacrificing himself willingly so that life can be reborn, and the bursting energy of springtime speaking joy to us with the return of new life and love.

When we integrate Shamanism into our worldview as witches, we deliberately dance the heartbeat and explore the energies of the world, and the realms that overlap with ours. We see the magical pathways in and out of these realms, and we go to them and we call them to us. When we cast the circle and go between the worlds, we are moving into the cosmos of the shaman, which is also the cosmos of the witch.

This section does assume that you have knowledge and experience in the Craft. I will assume that you have either dedicated yourself to the path of Wicca or have been initiated as a witch and priest or priestess in this spiritual path. I am not expecting years of experience or knowledge, but I am assuming that you have gathered your ritual tools, and regularly keep a Book of Shadows or other diary of your Craft activities. I will assume that you know the basics of wiccan ritual practice, and that you celebrate the Esbats and Sabbats. I will also assume that you have made your peace with the similarities and differences between Wicca and Witchcraft, and, even if you do not follow the Wiccan Rede, that you have an ethical statement that you follow with passion and integrity.

And now, as a witch, you hear the heartbeat of the drum. You pick up the drum and begin to dance the magical path of the Shamanic Witch.

We gathered together under the Dark Moon in celebration and exploration. The circle was cast and quarters called. The energy of the elements filled the circle with wisdom, knowledge, passion, and emotion. The power built as the Totems made their presence felt in a whisper, a song, and a great mystery. Three stood in the center and opened the portals to the Lower World and the circle grew, and then the same three opened the gates to the Upper World. Meeting in the center, magic arrived in thrilling sensation; goosebumps rose higher. The priestess raised her arms and called the Goddess into her; the priest stood humbly before the altar and became the God. The mystery of ritual solidified the power of the circle.

Embodying the Goddess and the God

The moon shone brightly above our circle. There was no drumbeat, but there might as well have been! Even though we were indoors, I could feel the pulsing of the land and the trees, almost like a gentle snore, as they slumbered in the winter landscape. I called to the Goddess of the Moon through the window to join our circle; to become one with me. And with a swift and enveloping influx of energy, I felt Her inside me. I heard Her inside my head, saying, "Whoohoo, this is fun—I like this body!" She wiggled a little bit, in a way I don't usually move. She began to speak and her voice came from my mouth. I felt such joy and compassion that seemed to reach to every corner of the Universe. I felt the elements in my being, even as I knew that I was still me—yet I was also Her.

The essence and focus of the practice of Wicca and Witchcraft is experiencing our interconnection with the Goddess and the God. Through these experiences and interactions, we become our true divine selves. Direct experience with the Goddess heals the separateness we feel between our body, our emotions, our mind, and our spirit, and heals the loneliness that we feel because we are separate from others. Direct experience with the God heals the separateness we feel to the nature that surrounds us, and closes the distance we feel to all the creatures that are part of this earth. In our experiences with the Goddess and the God, we learn that there is no separation and no loneliness, and that we are unified as an essential and vibrant part of the web of life and the Universe.

The practice of Wicca and Shamanism is a practice of the body. We are incarnate beings having a spiritual experience, and we are spiritual beings having a physical life. These are not religious practices that teach the celebrant to reject the body along with its pains and pleasures. We call our deities, spirit guides, and their energies to meld with ours both in spirit and in body. We see with their eyes, smell the same scents, and hear what they hear. Their heartbeats meld with ours when we seek and find the ecstasy of the Divine.

Even though the definition of ecstasy tells us that we move out of ourselves to another level of experience, that movement does not include rejecting any part of ourselves, and that includes our bodies. What we truly move away from is our sense of isolation and distance. Ecstasy is the experience of unity and union between ourselves and the transcendent Universe. To feel harmonious accord with every part of our being and to feel that same harmony with all that is in the Universe is ecstasy. To be ecstatic is to be a part of the One. We are the embodiment of wholeness and holiness. We can live in our bodies fully and with joy, understanding that every part of us is sacred. The idea is that we *are* sacred. The idea is *not* that we are sacred when we lose weight, when we have a full head of hair, or when we are buffed up! We are sacred now, in our bodies and in our current emotional state. Understanding the embodiment of divinity and living as sacred can be very tough to do in our culture.

We live in a culture that makes full embodiment very difficult. To achieve a bold and healthy sense of wholeness and union with our bodies requires that we run counter to most of our cultural assumptions. Messages from the media saturate our consciousness and are inculcated into lectures from our loved ones, health practitioners, and friends. If that were not enough, many of these messages are shaming and blaming, making us unable to accept our bodies as perfect and right in each moment. The ubiquity of a harmful, unrealistic body image makes it very difficult for us to accept our own bodies as normal, acceptable, and sacred. We must see ourselves as sacred consciously and constantly in opposition to very strong unconscious messages; messages that are wrong and make us feel dishonored. We can do it because we are witches and we are shamans. Our connections with the Goddess and the God and our active participation in our own spiritual lives allow us to go against this harmful flow of messages. We have the tools already.

The practice of grounding is one of those tools, and is essential to understanding what it means to be a Witch-Shaman. I spend a lot of time on different kinds of grounding in my teachings and in my writings because I believe it is essential to our growth as fully embodied spiritual beings, and because it is an important practice and tool in magical work. Grounding is a constant connection to the Mother Earth through our bodies, and is achieved through visualization and through conscious physical acts such as eating, drinking, dancing, and sex. Grounding serves to remind us that we are physical beings working and living in harmony with sacred realms and magical energies.

There are a number of ways to ground, connecting with the earth and the spirit of Mother Earth, and visualizations are highly effective. Visualizing yourself as a tree and sending roots downward into the earth is one way, and seeing yourself as a rock and melding yourself with the earth and soil is another. The connections created in grounding give you stability and serenity, qualities you need to cope with everyday life, including the big trials and the small tribulations that come your way. Below is a visualization meditation for grounding that I use frequently during rituals, during meditations, and in preparation for both magical work and my everyday life.

Grounding Visualization

Take a deep, centering breath, and let it out with a sigh. Take a second deep, centering breath and let it out with a loud noise, releasing tension, distraction, and other negative emotions as you make that noise. Take a third deep, centering breath and let it out with a tone (ommmmm).

As the last vibrations of that beautiful sound fades, see the vibrations and tones become colors inside you. Bubbles of colored light, swirling and twirling inside you. As you breathe deeply, see these colors swirl and twirl and fill your feet and legs, filling you and healing you. Breathe deeply, and see the colors swirl and twirl and fill your lower body, filling you and healing you.

This beautiful energy of color and light fills you and heals you; the magic of your energy fills your torso to your shoulders, swirling and twirling in beauty and joy, filling you and healing you. As you breathe deeply, you see the wonderful, beautiful colors swirl and twirl into your arms and down to the tips of your fingers, filling you and healing you. Filling you and healing you, beautiful, beautiful color.

As you breathe deeply, this beautiful color of you fills your neck and head, swirling and twirling, filling you and healing you. From the tips of your toes to the tips of your fingers to the top of your head, you are filled with the beautiful color of you, swirling and twirling, filling you and healing you. Take one deep, long, centering breath from the tips of your toes, to the tips of your fingers, to the top of your head, and fill yourself with the clear, bright, beautiful colors of your energy.

Cast your awareness down to your feet. Send roots down from your feet into the earth. Through whatever barriers of floors and into the earth, your roots go. Down, down into the earth. You feel the warmth of the earth surround you and guide you safely. Down, down into the earth you go. Find a place deep within the earth to anchor yourself. Loop your roots there, firmly but flexibly. Firmly but flexibly you are anchored.

Feel the energy of Mother Earth permeate your roots, and as you breathe deeply, the energy of the Mother moves upward to your feet. In your feet, the energy of the Mother dances and swirls with the energy of you, filling you and healing you. Together the energy of the Mother and the energy of you dance up your legs into your lower body, filling you and healing you.

As you breathe deeply, the dancing energy of the Mother and you dance and fill your torso and your shoulders, filling you and healing you. Dancing and swirling together, these two beautiful energies fill you. As you breathe deeply, the energy moves into your arms and hands, right down to the tips of your fingers, dancing and swirling together, filling you and healing you.

As you breathe deeply, this twinned and twined energy moves into your neck and your head, dancing and swirling, filling you and healing you. You are filled with the double energy of you and the Mother Earth from the tip of your toes to the tips of your fingers to the top of your head. Take one long, deep, centering breath, and feel the energy fill you from the tips of your toes, to the tips of your fingers, to the top of your head. You are filled with the wonderful, beautiful colors of the Mother Earth and you, dancing together in harmony.

As you breathe deeply, feel this doubled energy move out of your crown into the Universe above, moving upward in joy and love. Feel the energy of the Universe reach down to you, and hold you in its embrace. You feel loving abundance and power as you settle into the embrace. Feel the energy of the Universe move in harmony and union with the twinned energy of you and the Earth Mother. Feel this triad of energy move and dance in beauty and harmony.

Down, down this triple energy moves into your crown. The energy swirls together with your energy and the Earth's energy, filling you and healing you. Your head and neck are filled with this wonderful triple energy. As you breathe deeply, this energy moves into your shoulders and torso, swirling and twirling, filling you and healing you.

As you breathe deeply, this triple energy moves into your arms and hands, filling you and healing you. This magical combination of the loving Universe, the Earth Mother, and beautiful you fill you and heal you. As you breathe deeply, this triple energy moves into your lower body, filling you and healing you, swirling and twirling in magical, beautiful color and light. As you breathe deeply, the triple energy of you, the Mother Earth, and the loving Universe fills your legs and feet. This triad of energy fills you with warmth, love, and strength, filling you and healing you. You are filled from the top of your head, to the tips of your fingers, to the tips of your toes with this beautiful, warm energy of you, the Mother Earth, and the loving Universe.

Take a long, deep breath and feel this energy throughout your whole body. You are grounded in the love of the Mother, held in the embrace of the Universe, and held fast in the beauty of your own color and power. Take another deep breath and move your awareness into the here and now. Take a third deep breath and open your eyes.

I use this visualization in group rituals and meditations, and also in private devotions and daily practice. After doing this meditation as a practice, it becomes quick and easy. Your body becomes attuned to it, and responds to the visualization very quickly. You can also perform this visualization holding a talisman such as a stone, medallion, or piece of clothing. After grounding for several consecutive days while holding the talisman, you can then use it as grounding. Each time you pick up the talisman, hold it to your center or heart and breathe three times; you can ground without going through the more elaborate meditation.

Grounding and the Connection to the Worlds of the Shamanic Witch

This grounding meditation connects us to the earth below and also to the Universe above. I realized, after practicing this meditation for many years, that I could also actually connect myself to the Upper World and the Lower World as part of a grounding meditation. This helped make my shamanic journeywork more consciously connected to my work as a witch. I also believe that a variety of grounding meditations really helps each of us in all our circumstances. Sometimes, you just need to do something different!

The worlds of the shamanic practitioner are the worlds of the witch. They may be called different things, but they really are manifestations of the realms walked by the shaman and by the witch. The meditation below consciously connects the Witch-Shaman to all the realms. It builds on a regular practice of grounding and connection above and below. I generally do this grounding within a shamanic journeywork circle, or the cast circle of ritual. It is intended to open the passageways to deeper and clearer journeywork.

Stand comfortably with your feet on the ground, your knees bent slightly so that your body is flexible and comfortable. Close your eyes. Take a deep breath that fills you from the top of your head, to the tips of your fingers, to the tips of your toes. Let it out with a sigh. Take another long, deep breath, connecting all of your being. Let it out with a noise, letting go of any anxieties or stress. Take a third deep breath, and let it out with a tone (ommmmm).

As the vibrations of the tone fade away, take another long, deep breath, filling you fully with beautiful energy and light. Breathe deeply, and see this energy fully fill you. As you breathe deeply, you are filled with this beautiful color and light. This is the color of your embodiment. Breathe deeply into it.

From your feet, breathe in the energy of the Mother Earth and feel it fill you from the top of your head, to the tips of your fingers, to the tips of your toes. Breathe deeply the wonderful, beautiful energy of the earth. Feel it meld and dance with your energy in love and beauty. Take a long, deep breath.

From your crown, breathe in the energy of the Universe and feel it fill you from the top of your head, to the tips of your fingers, to the tips of your toes. Breathe deeply the wonderful, wise energy of the Universe. Breathe deeply and see this energy fully fill you. Feel it meld and dance with your energy in power and wisdom. Take a long, deep breath.

Take a long, deep breath and feel this triple energy meld together into an alchemical mix of magick and power. Breathe fully this wonderful energy.

Raise your arms upward, and stand as if you are a tree, wise and ancient. Connected to the earth, and with branches upraised to the heavens. Feel the flexibility of this tree as you sway slightly in the wind. Breathe deeply and become a tree. Cast your awareness down to your feet and see that there are roots there, going deep into the earth. Follow those roots downward into the earth, deep, deep into the earth. As you go down, down, deep into the earth, you feel the earth surround you. You feel the energy of the creatures living there. You find the anchor and stability of this tree, deep in the earth. As you move deep into the earth, you feel the energy change and shift. As the energy shifts and changes, you move into the Lower World, the realm of instinct and healing. You feel the difference as the energy moves downward.

As your awareness moves into the Lower World, breathe in the energy and connection. Find a place to anchor there. Breathe in the energy of the connection to the Lower World and feel it come upward into your being. Breathe.

Move your awareness to your head and arms. Feel your arms and fingers as branches, and move your awareness from your crown and the tips of your fingers upward into the sky. Feel the energy of the Universe in your awareness as you move upward. Breathe deeply as your awareness moves upward into the sky. As you move, you will find a permeable barrier, a light cloud, mist, or other gateway. Move through this and find your branches and awareness in the Upper World. Breathe in the energy of the Upper World. Breathe it inward into your being and feel that energy meld with the energies within you.

Breathe deeply from the tips of your toes and the ends of your roots. Breathe deeply from the top of your head to the end of your branches.

Take one long, deep breath and pull those energies into you. Feel that energy meld with the magick already inside you. Breathe deeply and see the energies of the Upper World and the Lower World meld with yours. Take one long, deep breath, and see the energies dance together in power, magick, and beauty. Take a deep breath and know that you are embodying all the worlds. Breathe deeply, and come back to the here and now. Breathe deeply and open your eyes, ready to journey.

The more we experience this magical work in our blood and our bones, the more connected we are not only to the world of Spirit, but to our own world as well. At first, our interactions with the creatures in this Middle World become more noticeable. Hawks swoop down out of the sky and rabbits hop into our awareness. If we live in cities, we notice—perhaps for the first time—that nature is all around us. The trees grow, plants and grass push their way up between cracks in sidewalks, and birds are everywhere!

After our awareness becomes heightened, we begin to see that the world around us has messages for us. Nature is talking all the time—we just need to learn to listen. Suddenly, it becomes apparent that there are messages and affirmations of our work. All the worlds reach out with messages for us. When I first moved into the house where I now live, I found feathers everywhere. Feathers on the campus where I work, feathers on my front porch, and feathers on my walks; messages from the natural world and the other worlds were literally dropping from the skies! The message I got was communication, communication, communication! Communication with intelligence and vitality was crucial for my still relatively new job. Communication with strength and without compromise was demanded for a relationship that was deteriorating. I acted on those messages and changed my life instead of letting the events in my life take command of me. It wasn't easy, and these kinds of helpful messages of insight are not intended to make our lives easier; accepting these messages, however, makes our lives more magical, manageable, and interconnected with all the worlds in which we work.

Grounding is an essential preparation for the central part of our work as witches, which is connection with the Divine. Our energies intermingle with the worlds of nature and magic, and we draw power and strength from those interactions. This kind of work is building our relationship with the Divine within us, the Divine that surrounds us in nature, and with the Divine beings that we call Goddess and God.

What every witch seeks is an energetic connection with the Goddess and God that is direct, personal, and real. We want to know that we can feel our connections and interactions as tangible experiences—as real and magical as those special, magical, ecstatic connections with ourselves and another person. It is love at its most basic and most mystical. This connection can be felt in sexual ecstasy, in spontaneous laughter, in a hug, and in a dish of chocolate ice cream. When we forget our concerns and problems, no matter how big or small, and merge into an experience, they are there. They are part of our skin, blood and bone, breath and thought. We become Goddess and God when we recognize that our own sacred connection to Deity is not a separate experience. They reach out to us from all the realms, but they also reach out to us from within our own beings. We must be fully embodied and aware to understand the affirmation of "Thou art God, thou art Goddess."

"I am Goddess, I am God," is a complex statement of self-acceptance and self-awareness. It is a complicated mix of gender issues, body image problems, emotions, and social issues. I have struggled with it in my life as a witch, and my students all struggle with the concept or parts of it. Because the statement is multifaceted, some parts are simple to accept, while others are very difficult. Our experiences and understanding of the world play a large part in how we embrace this concept. The messages we receive as children play a big part in how we accept the *fact* that each of us is a Goddess *and* God. It takes time, practice, and magic to not only understand intellectually that we are divine, but also to achieve that mystical understanding of our sacred nature; one that is part of the mystery of Wicca and Witchcraft and shamanic practice. Understanding that we are physical, embodied, and sacred is the work of a lifetime. The work of the Shamanic Witch is not only to understand that mystery for Self, but also to aid others in achieving this magical kind of knowing.

In my teaching, I spend a lot of time helping students understand that they are sacred before we begin to draw down the Goddess and embodying the Divine in other ways. Shamanic journeywork aids in the process of understanding that the whole of our divine and sacred selves is the work of a lifetime for embodied and incarnate humans. My partner, Mouse, calls this embodiment "learning to be truly human." To be truly human is to live completely in ourselves, intellectually, physically, emotionally, and spiritually, while at the same time knowing that we are connected to every other being in the world. We face and even embrace the best and worst of ourselves, and learn to understand ourselves without guilt or blame. By dealing with our weaknesses and working with our strengths, we find out who we truly are as human beings, and in acknowledging our humanness we also uncover and celebrate our own sacred selves.

To achieve this sacred embodiment, you have to do the work. It's all in the practice. Once the skills are learned, it is the ongoing connection through exercises, journeys, and rituals that keep us in our sacred and embodied state and bring us into an ecstatic union with the Goddess and God.

Reflecting Ourselves as Goddess and God

The mirror in my bathroom covers a whole wall. When I first moved in, I put a shelf in front of part of it because its ability to reflect all of me in this very intimate setting was overwhelming. It became the perfect place to find the Goddess within me. After my morning shower, instead of hurriedly going through my routine, I consciously stopped and stood in front of the mirror. I closed my eyes, took a deep breath, and connected with Mother Earth. I opened my eyes and looked into this very large mirror, and saw my naked self. I consciously moved criticism of my body aside, and just looked. I looked into my eyes; I looked at my hands, my feet, and the body in between. I took time and looked. When I was done, I met my eyes in the mirror and simply looked. I said, "You are Goddess." I then took another deep connecting breath, bowed and said, "I honor the Goddess that is in you and in me," and bowed again. I then turned out the light. I took a deep breath and came back to everyday consciousness, turned on the light, and started combing my hair, knowing that a shift had taken place.

How do we develop a practice that acknowledges and celebrates our own sacredness? Significant changes begin with small and continuous steps. In Wicca and Witchcraft and in shamanic practice, everyday objects become tools of power and wisdom as we use them in a magical context, and small acts of empowerment turn into large acts of magic and transformation.

The exercises and journeys in this section are very simple, and there are several variations in self-help books, empowerment books, and magic books. To understand that you are divine, you first have to convince yourself of that fact. The first exercise is to look in a mirror and to say, "I am Goddess. I am God." Then, go into a meditative state and wait for the wisdom to appear. On the surface, this may seem very simple and make sense intellectually, but this act is very significant for many people. In classes where I have done this, there have been women who will not look at themselves in the mirror, let alone say, "I am Goddess." When they finally get to the place where they can sit up straight and look in the mirror, it is an act of profound change. Adding a shamanic journeywork component is a truly magical transformation.

A mirror can become an important magical tool for the Witch-Shaman. Like the moon reflecting the light of the sun, a mirror reflects the light inside of us, if we let it. I will never forget one encounter I had with a mirror that changed my attitude about my appearance and my reflection. It was during a time when I was away from home on a business trip. It was in the first few months after I met Mouse, and I was deeply in love and excited about love. I sat down at the desk in my hotel room and called home to talk to him. As we were talking about this and that, I looked at the very large mirror over the desk, and instead of having my usual reaction about how ugly I look, I saw this glowing, beautiful woman who couldn't help smiling; the excitement and love was bursting though like sunshine and it was beautiful. Even I could look beyond my self-critical self and see the Goddess glowing from inside me!

Since that time, I have regarded mirrors in a very different way. If we allow our inner selves to show, the mirror is not the enemy, but one of the many gateways to find our own sacred and beautiful selves. A mirror as a magical tool can serve as a guide to show us where we are and how we need to change, as well as serve witness to the transformational work we are achieving.

Mirror Journey Exercises
Exercise One: I am Goddess and I am God

The first exercise is one that I just talked about, and that you can do with any mirror in your home. Just pick a place where you can stand for a couple of minutes, and make sure that you can at least see your face and shoulders. Decide beforehand what you will say. You can just say, "I am Goddess," or "I am God," or you can say, "I am Goddess and I am God." It depends on what internal messages you are working on.

Center yourself by singing or toning, and then take a deep breath and find your grounding by connecting with Mother Earth. Close your eyes, and take a deep breath. Do not forget to breathe. Open your eyes and say, "I am Goddess, I am God." Continue to look lovingly at yourself. You can repeat the phrase continuously or you can gaze in silence. When you are done, close your eyes and ground again. Repeat on a regular basis and as needed.

Exercise Two: Acknowledge and Honor the Goddess and God Within

This is the exercise described at the beginning of this section, and can be done either skyclad or clothed. As you incorporate this into a regular practice, you may decide at some point to move from clothed to skyclad. As a skyclad exercise, this moves you into body acceptance and wisdom, something very difficult for us in this society.

Use a mirror where you can view your whole body, in a place where you won't feel cramped and won't be disturbed. These practices are highly adaptable to your circumstances, so don't feel that the setting has to be completely ideal! Adapt, relax, and enjoy.

Stand in front of the mirror and gaze deeply at yourself. Close your eyes, and find your center by toning a single tone. Ground by finding your connection to Mother Earth, and with a long, deep breath, open your eyes. Don't forget to keep breathing. Look into the eyes of the person before you. Gaze lovingly at yourself, taking in your physical presence without criticism and judgment. Keep gazing and looking. When you are finished, put your hands in the Gasso, or prayer position, and bow deeply to yourself. Say, "I honor the Goddess and God within you. Blessed be." Close your eyes, and take a deep, grounding breath. Open your eyes and go about your day as the honored, sacred being that you are!

Exercise Three: Body Acceptance, Body Understanding

This exercise is done often in women's groups, and I wrote a ritual using a variation on an idea for Taurus in my book *Rituals of the Dark Moon: 13 Lunar Rites for a Magical Path*. I have done variations on this exercise alone and in groups. It never ceases to amaze me how deep and changing this can be. Even if you have done it before, each time new and deeper work is done. There is some wisdom that has to be done repeatedly to remind us that it is there and a part of us, so do not skip this one if you have done it before. Open yourself to new information and knowledge as you approach it again.

This exercise can be done clothed or skyclad, and in this case I highly recommend skyclad. Doing this exercise skyclad, either alone or with a trusted group, can forever change how you feel about your body and your own nudity. If you are not comfortable with a completely skyclad process, wear a robe so that you can look at your individual body parts. Whatever you do is right, and the important thing is that you are comfortable with the process of change. You should push your comfort levels slightly, not brutally!

You will be standing in front of a full-length mirror in a private, comfortable place in your home. Make this a special occasion and set aside some time to do it at a leisurely pace. Surround yourself with things that you love. If you are skyclad, be sure you are warm. (I once did this exercise wearing nothing but a pair of warm socks—it was a great look!) Play a drumming tape or soothing music. You might want to rattle or drum before beginning. Take a deep, cleansing breath, and ground thoroughly. Continue to breath, and open your eyes and begin.

Imagine that you are talking to the Goddess and telling Her in detail about your body. Start at the top of your head and move slowly downward. Be detailed and do not skip anything. Talk about your eyebrows, your teeth, your skin, your hair, your chin. Talk about your sexual parts, and talk about the things that are ignored liked calves, toes, and fingers. Don't miss anything. This process will be very emotional. Do not think about what you should say; say what you feel. If you hate your third toe on the right foot, talk to Her about it. Whatever you see in the mirror, talk to Her about it. You will be answering the following questions. Other thoughts will come up. Be sure to say them. Leave nothing unsaid. It is important for you to say it, for the Goddess to hear it, and for you to hear it. Our painful body experiences are one of the barriers to our belief in our own embodied divinity. Think about the following questions in relation to your body, and talk to the Goddess about your reflections.

- What is it?

- How does it serve me well?

- How does it not serve me?

- How does it feel?

- How does it make me feel?

For example, I would say: "Well, Lady, this is my left hand and it serves me well by writing, creating beautiful things like needlework, and doodling. There really isn't anywhere it does not serve me. It feels good when I flex it, and I'm thankful I don't have arthritis. I've always felt that left-handed people were interesting, magical, and creative, so my left hand makes me feel special." You can let stream of consciousness take over a little bit. No one will judge you because the only one listening is the loving Goddess. You might want to record the session, since often you will reveal hidden feelings and attitudes that are surprisingly important and wise. You will think, "I didn't know I felt that way!" You may find easy ways to make changes in your life because of attitudes hidden in your body. Even if it is not easy, you now have an awareness of how you feel and you can make the changes necessary to feel like the divine being that you are. This exercise is incredibly liberating and will change how you feel about your nakedness and about your body. Further on, you will find a ritual that builds on this work and moves you to the next step in embodiment, as you bless and celebrate your body.

When you are finished, breathe deeply and ground again, thoroughly connecting with Mother Earth. Leave your space and treat yourself well for the rest of the day. You have done some incredible work. Eat well, keep warm, and sleep well.

Shamanic Journey to Find Your Inner Goddess and Shamanic Journey to Find Your Inner God

These are two journeys structured the same way, and each has a different though similar intention. We live in a world of dualities and polarities, so we tend to see Deity in dual terms, of God and of Goddess. While on a Universal level, the reality may be of union and unity; in our bodies, we tend to look at the dualities. Of course, we all realize that the world is not just black and white, but that there are limitless variations, colors, and gray areas. The first time we do these journeys tends to reveal what we need to understand most. Subsequent journeys reveal the complexity and beauty of the dance with the Divine, and we find that God and Goddess are male and female, and so much more.

Take a hand mirror, big enough to see a large portion of your face, and go into your sacred space. Create beauty in this sacred space by creating an altar of things that you love and express who you are as a person. It is best to use a drumming tape or CD for this journey. Place the mirror on your altar, and call in the deities and spirits that you wish to witness and accompany you. Spend some time drumming and rattling, and then ground and center. This is a Middle World journey, where your power animal or animals will guide you.

Journey to Find My Inner Goddess

- When you are ready, settle into your space, taking the mirror with you.

- Put on the recording of drumming, and settle yourself comfortably for a trance.

- Gaze steadily into the mirror; after looking generally, stare in a focused way into your eyes.

- Call your power animal to help you and state your intention three times: "I call my power animal (name the animal) to guide me to find my inner Goddess."

- When you know that you can see your mirrored eyes with your eyes closed, close your eyes and begin the journey.

- When the call back is sounded, return to your space. Take a deep breath and open your eyes. Sit up and stretch.

Be sure to record the wisdom of your journey. If your inner Goddess did not tell you Her name, it will probably come to you at some point. In my first inner Goddess journey, She was the girl I wanted to be when I was young: smart, tomboyish, funny, active, and able to run swiftly. We climbed trees and talked about animals and books. In another journey, she appeared dressed as Xena: Warrior

Princess, an Amazonian character from a popular television show. This inner Goddess complained loudly about the costume, saying the other Gods were playing a joke by making her dress that way. Later, She revealed herself as the Goddess Artemis, Goddess of wilderness and the hunt.

Journey to Find My Inner God

+ When you are ready, settle into your space, taking the mirror with you.

+ Put on the recording of drumming, and settle yourself comfortably for a trance.

+ Gaze steadily into the mirror; after looking generally, stare in a focused way into your eyes.

+ Call your power animal to help you and state your intention three times: "I call my power animal (name the animal) to guide me to find my inner God."

+ When you know that you can see your mirrored eyes with your eyes closed, close your eyes and begin the journey.

+ When the call back is sounded, return to your space. Take a deep breath and open your eyes. Sit up and stretch.

Be sure to record the wisdom of your journey. If your inner God did not tell you His name, it will probably come to you through another journey or in a surprising "Eureka" moment. In my first inner God journey, the man that appeared to me dressed as the movie character Indiana Jones. As you can tell, popular culture icons play an important part in my journeys—I am a child of my culture! We had a fabulous adventure and a lot of fun. A few years later, he revealed himself as the God Dionysus, the God of the vine, ecstasy, agriculture, and theater.

The mirror exercises and journeys help us to understand our own divine natures and to heal the damage that has been done to our awareness. As we learn that we are divine creatures, we also see how society has damaged us. We may feel a great deal of anger and rage. It is important to acknowledge and understand these emotions, but not become fixated on them. The more we journey and work to become Witch-Shamans, the less we need the energy of these damaging emotions. We heal, and our scars give texture to our understanding; we find beauty as we move through pain to the other side.

Often, we will need to repeat the journeys and exercises, not because we did them wrong, but because each time we gain additional insight and depth. The emotion of betrayal was a big part of my life when I was younger, and there were many betrayals, large and small. As I worked through the events that led to those feelings and did journeywork to gain insight and tools, I found that the energy associated with the betrayals in my life had changed into understanding and forgiveness. I worked through the energy of betrayal and thought I had mastered it; I believed that I would never experience betrayal again. That was not true. I was betrayed in a relationship in a very dramatic way, but that time I wasn't focused on the emotion of betrayal; that time it was about working with grief. Earlier, at another point in my life, I would have focused on the lies and anger, but because I had done the dance, I was able to go deeper. It was not a repeat or do-over; this time, it was working on the important lesson of dealing with pain and sorrow. The intention of the journeys may seem repetitive, but we go further and deeper into wisdom and into the heart of the Goddess and God.

Melding with the Goddess and the God

The priestess drew the Full Moon Goddess into me before the full moon ritual began. She was there, ready to embrace these wonderful people and tell them of her love for them. Yet, they seemed to dither, and no one was willing to take charge of the ritual. Questions were being repeated, and no one took charge. Finally, the Goddess got annoyed— "Why did they call me here, if they aren't even going to listen?"—and yelled with my voice, "Okay, everybody, go downstairs and line up. Come up one at a time to meet the challenge of the Goddess." Startled, everyone moved downstairs. "This is more like it," I heard her whisper to me inside my brain.

One by one, they came up the stairs and received their challenge from the Goddess. As the ritual began with the circle cast and the quarter calls, I could feel her love grow and grow. Finally the center part of the ritual began, and she started talking to each participant, telling them what they needed to hear. I do not remember the words or what she said to each person. Even now, many years after the ritual, I remember first her annoyance and then her incredible, indescribable compassion for each one of the humans in the circle.

Up to this point, we have done inner work to acknowledge our own inner divinity and to celebrate our sacred natures. Now we move into greater connection with the world and with the Universe. It is this action that moves us outward into the Universe and into direct connection with the transcendent Divine, the sacred that infuses all nature and All That Is.

The Shamanic Witch walks and dances between the worlds and in connection with the Divine in two ways. One way, as we have discussed, is through the journeywork of the shamanic practitioner. Journeying to the Lower World, to the Upper World, and within our own Middle World reveals wisdom and healing to the Witch-Shaman. The Witch-Shaman learns to use this wisdom for the good of self and the good of all; these are acts of power and compassion.

The second way is through a variety of ritual and magical practices aimed at connecting and working with deities. Drawing down, invoking, channeling, possession, and aspecting are all things that the Shamanic Witch does to connect and dance with the Divine. All of these terms are aimed at explaining how disincarnate spirits connect and communicate through the body of a person. Combining these skills with shamanic journeywork moves the witch deeper into a connection with the Divine. When reading books on Wicca and Witchcraft and talking with other witches, it is clear that these terms have overlapping meanings depending on the traditions of the group and what authority is consulted. For the Witch-Shaman, these terms have layered and rich meanings.

Drawing down is practiced in pagan and Witchcraft traditions. Drawing down is usually done within a cast circle, and brings the deity or spirit into the body of a person, usually the High Priestess or High Priest. Most often, it is a full moon ceremony where the Full Moon Goddess is drawn down into the High Priestess by the High Priest. During Summer Solstice celebrations the Sun is drawn down into the celebrants or the Priest. This is done so the Goddess or God may speak directly to the circle of people. Another variation on this is drawing up the wisdom of the Earth Mother so that She may speak directly to the celebrants of the circle. These traditions are similar to the Oracles of ancient times, where people sought the wisdom and divination of the deities through a priestess or priest.

Invoking is the practice of inviting the Spirit or elemental force to enter the body of the priestess or celebrant. Gods, Goddesses, elemental spirits, spirits of place, and spirits of nature beings are all examples of invocations. Sometimes invoking happens spontaneously within a circle, where the celebrant will feel the Spirit enter them and speak through them. After one ritual, one of my coven sisters said of her experience of personifying the North, "It was me speaking, but it definitely wasn't me. There was another power present in my body, speaking with my voice." Some traditions have priestesses and priests with a special talent for invocation, and these special people make themselves available to their community. A person may ask the priestess to invoke a specific deity so that the seeker can ask questions and find wisdom.

Aspecting is a practice that is most often likened to drawing down. The seeker may decide to explore a particular characteristic of a deity, and bring that deity and that characteristic into themselves. For example, a woman may wish to explore the independent nature of Artemis and draw Artemis and independence into herself. Usually aspecting is done as part of a concentrated study of a particular deity. When seekers spend time immersed in the study of a deity or pantheon, aspecting is one of the ways to have a direct experience of the Goddess or God.

Possession is one of those freaky words that evoke gut responses based on some sensational stories and movies. Most often practiced by the Caribbean-Africana religions, possession is when the deity takes over the body and mind of the person. In Voudon and similar practices the person is said to have been "ridden" by the deity.

Channeling has become a New Age term describing when a person serves as a conduit for messages from a disincarnate being. Mediumship, or connection with the dead, is considered part of channeling. Wisdom comes from the mouth and body of a person, but another entity is talking and acting.

All of these terms describe skills and activities that connect us with all kinds of spirit beings. They are describing an embodied encounter with the worlds of Spirit. What is important to note is that there are different degrees of embodiment, in regard to how much of our own ego and personality are there within the experience. There are a number of ways of explaining it, and Judy Harrow, founder of the Proteus Coven, writer, and wiccan elder and leader, describes aspecting in four levels.[1] For the Shamanic Witch, these descriptions are very useful in developing a full understanding of embodied interactions of spirit entities.

Enhancement is lightest and closest to the normal state of mind. We are conscious and in control of our actions, but we sense things in a more intense fashion, and our language and gestures may become more poetic. In my experience, it is an added "oomph" and beauty to what is going on. I may be able to sing better than I normally do or remember things that I usually forget. It is a feeling of expansion and opening.

Inspiration is the second level of aspecting, and is where you begin to feel something more specific coming through you, including things you do not normally know or think about. You are still present in the experience, but you know for certain that someone else is there, guiding your words and actions. In my experiences, I know that I am there and that I am doing and saying things, but it is as if someone or something else is using my voice, hands, and body. I don't know who or what is coming through me; I just know that there is added wisdom, energy, and spirit in my actions and words. I have felt engaged, blessed, and energized by these experiences.

Integration is the third level, and some call it the actual state of aspecting. At this stage, the person actually speaks as God or Goddess. It feels like you have stepped aside to allow deity to use your voice and body. Afterward, the person may have some memory of what has occurred, but often there is no full memory. I usually retain the memory of the feelings. When I have done a drawing down of the full moon, I remember the emotions that were felt by the Goddess, but not the specific words. In my experiences, there has been one exception, and that is when I draw down or invoke the Dark Goddess at the Dark Moon. She instructs me as She speaks and acts, because, as She told me, the Dark Moon is my path.

Full trance possession is the fourth level of aspecting, where people do things they are not normally able to do, such as speak different languages, dance complex dances, and activities involving strength. There is no conscious memory afterward. It feels like you are tucked away in a safe place, and awakened later.

One of the most dramatic occasions for me was accidental, since I had no preconceived notion that it would happen. It was during a channeling exercise in a class I was teaching, and we were all lying within a cast circle. Our heads were all facing inward to the center of the circle, and as the exercise began, many of the people began softly speaking beautiful and gentle wisdom. I felt an enormous amount of exuberant, ecstatic energy come into me. The energy was pushing me to use my voice very loudly. I finally just stepped aside and my voice went "*Weeeeeeeehaaaaaaaa.*" It was Dionysus, God of wine and ecstasy and he had a lot to say. He decided to respect the circle and the expectations of others, but he really wanted to get up and dance while singing loudly. He contented himself with speaking loudly and, it turns out, wisely. The session was recorded and transcribed, and it all made sense in terms of a long conversation with the Goddesses and one high-spirited God. He also revealed that He was my inner God, and He was introducing Himself. In my personal practice, I acknowledge him as my patron God and work with Him often. As a matter of fact, much of my understanding of ecstasy as a spiritual practice comes from working with Dionysus.

Sometimes trying to define and describe experiences involving Spirit can be very difficult. While these definitions overlap and blur our intellectual understanding of our interconnection with the worlds of Spirit, it is our actual experiences that matter. In all of these definitions, it is not important what the experience is, but that you as the seeker know that you have had a valid experience and that you learn and grow from it. The point of understanding our embodied interactions with the Goddess and God is to enrich our experience of the moment when it happens. We can think about it all we want, but until it happens we don't know it in our blood, bones, and skin.

These embodied experiences are part of the ecstasy experienced by the Shamanic Witch. The ecstatic practices of Wicca and Witchcraft are very shamanic because they move us out of our separate selves into unity with the Universe. Our staid measured steps and planning are transformed into a dance with the Divine.

As practitioners, priestesses, and priests, we are not at the mercy of spontaneous experiences because we actively develop the skills needed to intentionally achieve these experiences. By developing our skills through practice and study, we ready ourselves to step deliberately into ecstasy. With intention and skill, we walk all the worlds of the spiritual and material planes and we find that we know the steps of our ecstatic dance.

Preparing for Melding with the Divine

One of the ways to prepare for aspecting and other channeling experiences is to be ready; to make sure that you, as a witch and shamanic practitioner, have an ongoing wiccan and shamanic practice where you are able to move between the worlds and experience your journeys; and, that you are comfortable with wiccan ritual and work well within the flow of universal energy. As you do this, as a person you become stronger, more openhearted, more compassionate, and more sensitive to the energies around you; as a Witch-Shaman, you become wiser and more powerful. The steps you take in your routine practices continue to clear passageways of power within you. Deity will want to come for a visit!

I began to deliberately seek communion and union with the Divine through guided visualizations. I developed meditations where I merged with specific Goddesses so that I might understand Her or aspects of her more fully and more deeply. What works best for me is to do a guided visualization as part of a drumming journey, combining shamanic skills with wiccan ones. I included devotional worship in the process, which included altar devotions. I took care to research the Goddess with whom I was working. I knew Her stories and what other people said about her. I spent some time thinking about Her and what role She might have played in my life so far. I would take a couple of the stories that spoke to me the loudest and rewrite them. I did this because I feel that sometimes the Goddess stories that come down to us through history have political and sociological slants to them that are not relevant to me as a person in this day and time. I would write the stories so that they had meaning to me as someone seeking the wisdom of this Goddess. Then I would guide myself through a visualization where I met with her, and had her meld with me so that I could seek her wisdom. I have often combined it with another familiar practice, such as working with the chakras, so that there is a context for the information to come from the Goddess. Below is such a meditation ceremony, written so you can substitute the Goddess or God of your choice.

Meditation Ceremony to Meld
with the Goddess or God

There were probably one hundred women in the Saturday night workshop. They were excited and ready to explore. The excitement grew as we sang our names and laughed. We talked about this lovely and strong Goddess, and began to go into meditative space. Most were standing as they stood like the Goddess, ready to dance. As I began the meditation, my goosebumps rose as the women met the Goddess. Then, with an extraordinary swooping feeling that felt like "Whomp!", I could feel the Goddess meld with all of the women. As the meditation moved forward, the women began to sway and move as the Goddess moved in joy. When the meditation was over, we shared a sweet, spicy drink; then, we raised a cone of power to move the ecstasy into the Universe in celebration of Her. The workshop was over, and every woman left to go to drumming and dancing, full of ecstasy and love.

Prepare your understanding; research the Goddess or God, noting the stories and legends. Spend some time looking at both archaeological and artistic images of this deity. Keep them in your thoughts and other spiritual activities as you work to know them. Know what foods, objects, and creatures are sacred to them. Write poems and stories about them and to them. Create invocations as you immerse yourself in the experience. You will probably find that appropriate objects will find their way into your possession through amazing synchronicity!

Prepare your ritual space by creating an altar to this specific deity. Use images and objects sacred to Her or Him. Be sure to have incense, candle, water, and salt as tools relating to the four directions so that you can do the altar devotion. Use candles and incense to create a relaxed atmosphere. In this case, a drumming tape or CD is appropriate, unless you are adept at journeying and meditating while drumming. The best way to do the meditation is to be standing, so that you can move and sway with the power that has entered you.

Ground and center yourself. Imagine your space surrounded by a clear blue light of protection. Go to the altar for the altar devotion. Substitute the name of your particular deity for "Goddess" in this ceremony.

Take a deep breath of connection, bow your head, and say: "Before this altar dedicated to the Goddess, I say my devotions to Her. My body, spirit, and mind is open to Her wisdom."

Light the incense, and move your hand into the smoke so that it moves over your body, and say, "I breathe in the breath of the

Goddess. I cast all negativity to the winds of change that I may be cleansed in Her intuition."

Light the candle and move your hand over the flame so that the heat moves toward your body, and say, "I feel the passion of the Goddess. I cast all negativity to the fires of change that I may be cleansed in her vitality."

Dip your hands in the water and sprinkle it over you, and say, "I bathe in the heart of the Goddess. I cast all negativity into the well of change that I maybe cleansed by Her love."

Take some of the salt and sprinkle it over you, and say, "I stand in presence of the Goddess. I cast all negativity into the earth that I may be cleansed in her dark silence."

Move your hand deosil over all the elements and say, "By air, fire, water, earth and by intuition, passion, love, and dark silence, I am a vessel of the Goddess."

Take a deep breath and settle yourself into a comfortable position for meditation. Turn on the drumming tape and take a long, deep, cleansing breath.

Take a deep breath and close your eyes. Take a long, deep breath that moves the energy inside you from the tips of your toes, to the tips of your fingers, and to the top of your head. As you breathe deeply, find your connection to Mother Earth and to the Universe above. Breathe deeply, and move into trance.

You are standing in your favorite outdoor space. You breathe in the love and beauty of this space as you feel the energy of the space fill you with wonder.

(pause)

As you look around and drink in the peace of this place, you notice a pathway leading to the west. You go to the pathway and begin to follow it as it begins to curve downward. You notice the path and what it is made of as you move downward.

(pause)

You notice the surroundings as you move deeper and downward. Appearing before you is your power animal as you move deeper along the path. Your power animal speaks and begins to guide you deeper along the path.

(pause)

You come to a clearing or circular place at the end of the path. Your power animal guides you to the southern edge of this circle.

(pause)

Drumming begins and you hear music as you breathe deeply the energy of this place. As the drumming and music intensifies, a group of people dance into the center of the circle. They are riotous and exuberant in their dance. They laugh and sing, and there are lots of floating and swirling fabrics in rich, vibrant colors.

(long pause)

One of the dancers catches your attention and you watch that One for a long time.

(long pause)

That One looks over to the South and sees you sitting there, and comes over to you and sits beside you. The One speaks to you and you listen.

(pause)

The One tells you to stand up and you do. As you stand facing one another, the One takes a deep breath and moves into your body, and the two of you are melded together. As you breathe deeply, you feel the energy of this One within you. You begin to move and sway with the energy of the One inside you.

(long, long pause)

As you are standing there, your combined awareness focuses on your body and your physical life. You will find insights and wisdom about how you feel about your material life. Wisdom about money, belonging, and survival will come to you as you listen, moving and swaying.

(long pause)

Slowly, your combined awareness focuses on your emotions and feelings as you find insights on the emotions that rule your life. What needs to be strengthened, what needs to be hanged, what needs to be lost, and what needs to be gained will come to you as you listen, moving and swaying.

(long pause)

Slowly, your combined awareness focuses on power, work, recognition, and attainment; how you relate to the power of the Universe on the planes of existence. What needs to be done, what needs to stop, what understanding is needed, and how you move in the flow of the Universe will come to you as you listen, moving and swaying.

(long pause)

Slowly, your combined awareness will focus on the matters dear to your heart, who you love, your humanity, charity, and compassion.

What needs to change, what needs to open, what needs to be lost, and what needs to move to another will come to you as you listen, moving and swaying.

(long pause)

Slowly, your combined awareness will focus on how you express yourself and how your inner life shines outward for others to see. What needs to change, what habits and expressions serve you well, what causes you pain, what inhibits you, and what gives you joy will come to you as you listen, moving and swaying.

(long pause)

Slowly, your combined awareness will focus on your intuition and magic and how your connection with divine wisdom, both innate and external, manifest. What needs to change, what needs to strengthen, what needs to grow, what serves you well, and what helps you shine will come to you as you listen, moving and swaying.

(long pause)

Slowly, your combined awareness will focus on your divinity and connection with the Divine Universe. What needs to change, what needs to open, and what needs to be understood will all come to you as you listen, moving and swaying.

(long pause)

Finally, your combined awareness will see you as whole and holy; how you shine together, and how you move and sway in harmony with the Universe. You move and dance together, two in one, One and Two. You feel belonging, love, connection, compassion, beauty, magic, and wisdom as you move together in love, harmony, and ecstasy.

(long pause—move, move, move)

And now it is time to go your separate ways, knowing that this feeling lingers in the interconnectedness of life. The One moves outside of you and faces you. You hold hands and say your good-byes. With a deep breath and a kiss, the One moves back into the swirling dance. Your power animal comes to you and guides you back up the path. Up you go toward your favorite outdoor place. Up and up until you are standing in the center of that beloved place. With one deep breath, you come back to the present time. With a second breath, you return to your space, and with a third breath, you open your eyes.

Be sure to record the wisdom of the meditation, along with the ceremony. As a Witch-Shaman, recording the wisdom of your journeys is an important part of regular practice. You may also find other ways of expressing the journey, including song and dance.

Bid farewell to the One who joined you. At your altar, say good-bye and thanks to the elements assembled there. Cast your awareness to the blue light surrounding your space, and see it fade slowly into clearness and meld with the air around you.

Be sure to ground in meditation, and by eating something nourishing. This kind of work takes a lot out of you, and you will need to replenish your energy.

The best setting to practice melding with the deities is within the ritual. In ritual, the space is prepared and protected. Within a cast circle is a safe, cleansed, and purified container for the magic to happen. In stories to follow, you will find rituals for invoking and melding with the sacred Divine, and you will experience how your own sacred being joins in a dance with the sacred Ones.

Drawing Down the Moon
Ritual for Invoking and Aspecting the Goddess in Celebration of the Full Moon

This ritual explores embodying the Goddess by using the skill of aspecting. In this ritual, you will draw down the Goddess into your body, for the stated intended purpose to seek Her wisdom on what gifts the full moon brings to you and your assembled circle.

This ritual can be done indoors or outdoors, at night close to when the full moon has risen in the sky. Do this ritual during the phase of the full moon or the waxing moon. Be aware that when you draw down the Goddess, you draw down the aspects of Her that are present in the Universe and in your intention. Waning and dark moon aspecting is done after a lot of practice, because the Dark Goddess is made of stern stuff. She loves us, and shows this love to us by making us face some hard and cold facts.

I use drums and rattles in these kinds of ritual to heighten the meditative awareness and to help move me and others deeper into meditation. I often drum the heartbeat rhythm during the circle casts and quarter calls. If you are alone, you can put on a drumming tape or CD to be played during the ritual. Keep it low so the sound is in the background.

Create Sacred Space: Get your space ready by cleaning it and preparing it for your sacred Divine Guest. You will be doing a cleansing and purifying as part of the ritual. Set up your altar with your tools and adorn it with beautiful decorations. Use images of the moons, and silver colored candles and ornaments. Seasonal flowers and other decorations also enhance the beauty of the altar.

Altar Devotion: Light the incense and move your hand into the smoke so that it moves over your body, and say, "I breathe in the breath of the Goddess. I cast all negativity to the winds of change that I may be cleansed in Her intuition."

Light the candle and move your hand over the flame so that the heat moves toward your body, and say, "I feel the passion of the Goddess. I cast all negativity to the fires of change that I may be cleansed in her vitality."

Dip your hands in the water and sprinkle it over you, and say, "I bathe in the heart of the Goddess. I cast all negativity into the well of change that I maybe cleansed by Her love."

Take some of the salt and sprinkle it over you, and say, "I stand in presence of the Goddess. I cast all negativity into the earth that I may be cleansed in her dark silence."

Move your hand deosil over all the elements and say, "By air, fire, water, earth and by intuition, passion, love, and dark silence, I am a vessel of the Goddess."

Cleanse the Circle: Add salt to the chalice, and move widdershins around the circle, chanting, "By salt and water, this circle is cleansed."

Purify the Circle: Light incense, and move widdershins around the circle, chanting, "By air and fire, this circle is cleansed."

Cast the Circle: Begin in the North and, with athame pointed to the ground, walk around the circle with the following words. If you finish before you reach the North, walk in silence.

> I conjure now the powers of dark and light
> Encircle us with love, clear and bright.
> Move us into time-no-time
> Between the worlds of place-no-place
> Where magick is born and wonder happens.

Beginning at the North, walk deosil and hold the athame at shoulder length, and chant:

> By the power of my hand, I cast the magick
> circle round
> To create a shield, shining bright, to protect,
> defend, and guard us.
> From North, South, East and West, we call
> blessings to this place.
>
> By roots and rocks we call below
> To the beauty of the earth
> Into our circle flow.
> By the stars in the darkened sky
> We call magick, come, into our circle fly.

Starting at the North, hold the athame in the air with one hand and the other hand to the ground, and say:

> Hail to the powers of the starry Heavens
> Surround and protect us this dark sacred night
> Keep us safe 'till the dawn of the bright blessed day.

Open our souls to see beyond the Veil
To greet the ancestors of blood and bone, heart
and soul.

Stand at the North, holding the athame high in one hand and the other hand to the ground. Stomp your foot, and chant:

By the full moon and by sweet earth,
this circle is sealed.
We are between the worlds.
Blessed be!

Center and Ground: In silence, find your connection to Mother Earth and bring that energy into your body. When that energy begins to move and dance with yours, move your awareness out of the crown of your head, and find connection with the Universe. Take one long, deep breath from the top of your head, to the tips of your fingers, to the tips of your toes. Know that you are centered and grounded.

Call the Quarters:

North:

By the powers of strength and silence,
I call you, Bear, guardian of rich earth.
Come foundation, come stability, come Gnome
Bring your protection, mighty North.
Hail and welcome.

East:

By the powers of mind and intuition,
I call you, Robin, creature of song.

Come innocence, come joy, come Sylph
Bring your brightness, sweet East.
Hail and welcome.

South:

By the powers of purpose and intention,
I call you, Cheetah, moving with determination.
Come will, come persistence, come Salamander
Bring your power, mighty South.
Hail and welcome.

West:

By the powers of healing and love,
I call you, Otter, playing in the sea.
Come heart, come feeling, come Undines
Bring your soul, loving West.
Hail and welcome.

Center:

By the powers of union and connection,
I call you, Eagle, farseeing and wise
Fly from Above and into the Center fly;
I call you, Snake, changing and wise,
Move from Below and into the Center come.
Wisdom and mystery, rise and flow
Meet in the center with magic and love.
Hail and welcome.

Call to the God or Goddess:

Call the Goddess:

> Lady of the moon, bright and full,
> I call you to come, come to the circle.
> In the light of fullness and joy
> Bring your wisdom, and bring your gifts.
> Beloved Lady, hail and welcome.

Call the God:

> Lord of the hunt, Consort of the Lady,
> I call you to come, come to the circle.
> Bring your wildness, your power and delight.
> Lord of the Wild Ones, hail and welcome.

Statement of Ritual Intent: Drum yourself into a meditative state. Call your power animals to you, acknowledging the totems in your midst. State the intention three times: "I call my power animal to me, and I will draw the Goddess into myself. I will meld with Her and ask her wisdom and gifts for this full moon night."

Draw Down the Goddess: Stand before the altar, raise your hands, and call to Her. When you feel Her energy come down through your crown and fill your whole body, lower your arms. Turn and face the center of the circle, and begin to speak Her wisdom. If you are alone, you may want to have a recorder on hand.

> Lady of the full moon, beloved Goddess,
> Enter into me and be One with me here.
> In mystery and magick, I call you to join me.

See with my eyes, hear with my ears,

Embrace love with my arms,

And walk the path of wisdom with my feet.

Love with my heart and join me here.

Come now and blessed be!

Turn and speak Her wisdom. When it is time, and you will know it, turn back to the altar and say your farewells.

Blessed Lady, love, and mystery,

With thanks I bid you farewell.

Go from my body, and linger in this space.

Blessings to you beloved Lady.

Go now and blessed be!

I usually blow Her a kiss as she leaves my body. Spend a minute thinking of the gifts She brought to the circle.

Raise a Cone of Power: If She gave you a word or phrase, use that in raising a cone of power. Otherwise, use a tone that begins very low and make it louder and faster until it moves off into the Universe with a whoosh. Feel the energy move through your body and out through your hands as the whoosh goes toward your intention, to understand the gifts the Goddess has for you.

Ground and Center: Take a moment to reconnect to the energy of Mother Earth. Feel your connection to the Universe. Gently move any energy that you have extended outward back into your body. Know that you are always grounded whenever you step on the earth, and you are always connected to the Universe whenever you look into the sky.

Farewell to the God:

> Great Lord, mighty Hunter,
> Thank you for the great love you hold
> For us and for Your Lady.
> Go with our thanks and our blessings.
> Hail and farewell.

Farewell to the Goddess:

> Loving Mother, gracious Goddess
> Thank you for your gifts, your presence,
> And the wonders that you bring to us
> Body and soul.
> Go with our thanks and our blessings.
> Hail and farewell.

Dismiss the Quarters:

Center:

> Fare thee well Eagle and Snake,
> Above and Below
> In perfect trust from us go.
> Hail and farewell.

West:

> Fare thee well, magical West,
> Otter and Undines
> In perfect trust from us go.
> Hail and farewell.

South:

> Fare thee well, passionate South,
> Cheetah and Salamanders

In perfect trust from us go.
Hail and farewell.

East:

Fare thee well, knowing East
Robin and Sylphs
In perfect trust from us go.
Hail and farewell.

North:

Fare thee well, silent North
Bear and Gnomes
In perfect trust from us go.
Hail and farewell.

Take up the circle: Walk widdershins around the circle, pointing your athame down toward the earth. Visualize the circle being taken into your athame. At the North, point the knife downward and allow the energy to go back into Mother Earth.

Standing in the Body of the Goddess and the God: Trance Posture Meditations

We were standing in the posture of Bear, based on an ancient figurine of a bear. It was hot, and we were out in the middle of a field in the mid-day summer sun. It was difficult to maintain this posture. Suddenly, as I breathed, I felt a big ball of golden light come from my center and move outward. I was filled with golden light; the discomfort disappeared as I was transported to the sun. I felt the glorious energy and passion of the sun, and I was filled with the beauty of the world. I just moved on that energy for a very long time. We were called back to the circle, and I was back in the hot field with a big fly buzzing around my head. It did not seem to matter, as I was still buzzing with the ecstatic energy of the sun.

Some of the most powerful meditations for the magical practitioner are the ones that involve the body; moving meditations such as labyrinth walking, Tai Chi, Karate, and Dances of Universal Peace, as well as rhythmic walking, swimming, and running are all ways of communion with the Divine. The whole body is engaged and becomes an instrument and container for divine wisdom that comes both from within and from a transcendent source. The body melds with Spirit in speechless wonder as we experience the sacred, right down to our bones and blood.

Trance posture meditations are a shamanic practice based on the work of Felicitas Goodman[2], an anthropologist who studied the effect of trance on the body. She discovered that as people stood in the postures of ancient deity figurines, they experienced profound journeys, and not only did they move outside of themselves to dance ecstatically with Spirit, they also experienced some things in common with other journeyers using the same posture.

Our bodies somehow remember and retrieve ancient memories and experiences. At the time I discovered this idea, there were not many books on the subject. It occurred to me that if I stood in a posture similar to that of a Goddess statue, whether ancient or modern, it might be an interesting experience. Was I ever right there! Standing in the posture of Inanna holding her breasts or Kuan Yin in the Royal Ease posture was truly and profoundly life changing. The journeys those postures brought me were exceptionally wise. I truly experienced what it meant to say, "I am Goddess."

Journeying while in those Goddess postures has helped me move into body awareness, acceptance, and enjoyment.

On a number of occasions, I have led a workshop called, "Standing in the Body of the Goddess." I chose two Goddess figurines and statues I thought were universally recognized and understood. As usual, when teaching, I learn a lot, and one of the things I learned was not to assume that anything is universally recognized. The first time I taught the workshop, it was scheduled early on a spring Sunday morning, which happened to be the Sunday the time moved forward an hour. Only one woman showed up at the large hotel meeting room. The room was all mirrors and gilt furniture, with a carpet pattern that was overwhelmingly awful—it actually made me dizzy. The very nice woman in the workshop did not know the two Goddesses, and I had not brought any pictures. Nevertheless, we both bravely went on with the workshop in the midst of the brash décor.

I described the Venus of Willendorf, with her large round body, pendulous breasts, and tiny feet. I had the woman stand in the posture of the Goddess, with her legs bent and her hands on her thighs. I drummed for about twenty minutes, and I could feel the tingling sensation that I get when something incredible is happening in circle. Afterward, the woman's description of her journey was ecstatic. She felt abundance, fertility, and a sense of rightness about her physical being. She felt *there* in her body.

For the Snake Goddess of Crete, I had her face a mirror and hold her hands up and imagine she was holding a snake in each hand. I described the Goddess to her, and asked her to assume the Goddess position. I stood behind her and drummed, and this time I journeyed as well. At one point, I opened my eyes and looked ahead, and I could see this wonderful woman standing there as Goddess. I was behind her, holding my drum upright in a similar position, and I could see lines and lines of strong, powerful women dancing and standing in power. They were not just standing in power, but also claiming power as their birthright. The woman told me that this was very moving for her. Since she was small in stature, she had never felt very strong or powerful, but this journey made her feel big, strong, and full of power in a way that she had never felt before. She hugged me and said, "I will remember this."

Journeys: Standing in the Body of the Goddess and God

This journey can be done with any statue or posture of a Goddess or God. I chose ones that are fairly well-known. Feel free to use photographs and props to help you get into the spirit of the journey; I have also found it helpful to research the Goddess or God whose statue or posture you are using before the journey. Be sure to prepare your space as sacred. Use a drumming or rattling tape, or have someone drum or rattle for you. Rattling is especially effective in trance journeywork. If standing for fifteen or twenty minutes is not possible for you, sitting and using your upper body in the posture is just as effective. Often, lying down in that posture is nearly as effective as standing.

Trance Journey in the Posture of the Venus of Willendorf

Stand in the posture of the Venus of Willendorf. Stand with your knees slightly bent. With this figure, it is not clear where her arms are, so hold them in front of you with your hands at your sides or on your thighs. Breathe deeply, and close your eyes. Keep breathing and allow the drum and rattle to take you on this journey.

Trance Journey in the Posture of the Snake Goddess of Crete

Stand in the posture of the Snake Goddess of Crete. Stand with your feet firmly apart and your knees slightly bent. Straighten your back, and lift your arms up and close your hands as if you are holding two snakes (you may want to use rubber snakes for this). Hold your head like you are balancing a cat on your crown. Breathe deeply, and close your eyes. Keep breathing and allow the drum and rattle to take you on this journey.

Trance Journey in the Posture of the Horned God
Figure 3: The Horned God

Stand with your legs a shoulder width apart. Bend your knees slightly and place your hands on the front of your thighs. Keep your back straight, as if you have two horns coming from your head. Breathe deeply, and close your eyes. Keep breathing and allow the drum or rattle to take you on this journey.

These are a few examples of the trance journeys that you can take. You can use drawings, photographs of statues, and figurines. I have found this kind of journey to be a deep communion with the Goddess and the God; a physical way to experience Them as part of my own being, and a way to experience the interconnectedness of all life. It is a great way to understand Them as who they truly are.

Rituals in Shamanic Wicca:
The Sacred Space and Time

Ritual is the central practice of Wicca and Witchcraft; it is the activity that links all the separate explorations and practices into an integrated experience and interactions with the spirits of all the worlds and us, the humans. In Wicca, ritual has a central and common format. Moreover, other practices such as spellwork, healing, and energy work have a ritualized aspect to them. We work in harmony with the flow of energy that we create, and then, as powerful Witch-Shamans, we move it onward toward our own goal, which is now in concert with the Universe.

Ritual is set in sacred space and time where there is no space and time. It is what I call the place-of-no-place and the time-of-no-time. We move intentionally into this sacredness between the worlds to work with disincarnate beings, the world of elements, the Ancestors, and the Divine. We celebrate, work magic, create change, and learn to be who we are as sacred beings. We learn to stop doing, and we learn to just be.

The Circle is Cast and We are Between the Worlds

In the circles where I celebrate ritual, we almost always say, "The circle is cast, and we are between the worlds," or some phrase similar to that. What does that mean? Does it mean that, like in some science fiction movies, we are in some kind of limbo land where nothing is there? Does it mean we are "beamed" outside of our ordinary world to some other place? I have experienced it many times, as well as thought about it for a long time.

When we cast a circle, we move envisioned energy in a circle, usually traveling in a sunwise or deosil direction, and then we envision the energy moving underneath us, and then moving above us. We are enclosed in a sphere of our own energetic making, and what we do is cast our energy outward in the four cardinal directions into the Middle World. We then move our energy downward into the overlapping Lower World, and then we move our energy upward into the Upper World. It is accurate but imprecise to say that we are slicing out sections of the Middle, Lower, and Upper worlds. We move them outside of time and place for the stated purpose of the ritual. In my experiences, the energetic casting of the circle does not have the invasive implications the word "slicing" might have. We are consciously melding the overlap of the three worlds together and temporarily moving that section, circle, or sphere to a destination outside of time and place.

Once we move outside of temporal concerns, we then call on the sacred beings of all three worlds to be a part of the work we are about to do. We ask them to come to us in a variety of aspects and ways. Casting a circle and doing a ritual is an action full of intent, just as a successful journey is focused on an intention. In a shamanic journey, we travel outward to build relationships with the creatures and spirits of the magical realms; in a cast circle we invite them to be partners in making our intentions successful.

I think that within a cast circle we actually do both; travel outward to seek the wisdom of the spirits, and ask the spirits to come to us for a specific purpose. Many rituals are based in meditations and trance. Some meditations move us deep within ourselves, where we explore our own emotions and our bodies; other meditations take us to another place to gain wisdom. Each time, those meditations seek the wisdom of the sacred, which exists both within and outside us.

The shamanic circle ritual I mentioned earlier does not cast a circle. In the circle that I facilitate, many of the participants are not wiccan or even identify themselves as pagan, so it would be inappropriate and insensitive to cast a circle in that situation. Even so, we work in a circle, and by calling in the spirits and creatures of the six directions we make ourselves separate from our ordinary lives, though without the discrete separations of a cast circle. Without the distinction of a cast circle, the edges between the circle and all the worlds are blurred and nebulous. This can be both a weakness and a strength. Participants may come and go from the circle without cutting a doorway, but this and other outer distractions may weaken the circle more quickly, and both the participants and the spirits called into the circle may find their concentration waning.

In this case, what holds the center and the circle is the power of the drum and the rattle. The drum, the drumming, and the drummer can be so powerful and compelling that the circle is held intact because the unity of the drummer with the drum pulls and holds the attention of all the spirit and embodied participants. As in other circles and rituals, everyone present is an active participant and holds responsibility for maintaining the circle's integrity.

There are times when practicing wiccans and witches find it appropriate to use this kind of circle rather than a formally cast circle. Often when I read Tarot cards for someone or when I teach or when a group is gathering together for a circle meeting or other activity rather than ritual, a less formal circle is appropriate. The nebulous circle heightens our awareness of the sacredness of the activity, but also allows us to direct our energy to a work that requires the skills of our everyday awareness.

An example of this kind of circle cast is something I call the classroom circle cast. It does not have a fancier name because it is a very workable, workday kind of casting that helps me remember that everything I do is sacred and magical. You can create this kind of circle by taking the following steps.

- Create a group attunement by toning a syllable. Often I use "Ma," which reminds us of Mother Earth.

- Breathe into the center of your beings.

- Find your connection to the Mother Earth using a grounding visualization.

- Return to the first attuning tone.

This is a short and simple way to create a circle with a center but not formally cast one between the worlds. It emphasizes the holiness of the work, while at the same time allowing everyone access to this world as an anchor and frame of reference. They are centered and prepared for the work ahead.

How the Shamanic Witch Does Ritual

One of the first places to look when blending the practices of Shamanism and Wicca is in ritual. Ritual is the cornerstone and bedrock of Wicca and Witchcraft. Ritual is the place where the witch deliberately goes to commune with the Gods and the spirits of all realms. Ritual creates a space to celebrate, to create change, and to find information. Sometimes when something serious needs attention and some intense work, a ritual is created and enacted that will put the ritual intention into motion in harmony with the flow of universal energy. Healing, divination questions, spells, celebrations, and life passage ceremonies are all times when a formal ritual between the worlds is needed.

One of the strongest shamanic aspects of Wicca is working with totems for the directions. In my wiccan tradition, we have totems for East, South, West, North, Above, and Below. We open the portals to the Upper and Lower Worlds in the center, and all the energies are melded there, creating a dynamic, fertile, and transforming environment within the cast circle. Because everyone in our tradition works with these totems and uses the same quarter calls and circle casting, the magic increases and becomes alive in the Middle World, the Lower World, and the Upper World. As members continue to meditate and journey with these totems and then call them into circle, a strong relationship is created and maintained.

Choosing and Working with Totems

More often than not, your totems choose you. You may spontaneously merge with a totem in a meditation or ritual, or the totem may appear and tell you that it is the totem you are seeking. In other cases, there may be energies and animals that you wish to work with over a long period of time. It is a good idea to already be familiar with and to be working with the energies of the directions and the elements before choosing totems for open rituals. On the other hand, having experience and understanding is important; do not be frozen into inaction by worrying too much about what goes wrong. The spirits want to work with you, and they also want you to be smart about what you are doing. Balance is always the key.

For my public work and open circle rituals, I started working with totems for each of the directions; I took multiple approaches, ones that I called the intellectual approach, the embodied approach, and the spiritual approach. They can be used in any order, and in this case I began with the intellectual approach.

First, I thought about the interplay of energies in the directions and the elements; then, I thought about the deeper energies that I wanted to work with over the long-term. For East, I wanted to discover innocence and how to give voice; for South, I wanted to explore the application of will and persistence; for West, I wanted to look at opening the heart and soul; for North, I wanted to explore connecting to the stability and foundation of Mother Earth. I moved into thinking about Above and Below, and explicitly connecting to the energies of the Upper and Lower Worlds. For Above, I wanted to celebrate the wisdom, and for Below, I wanted to affirm my connection to the mystery.

I developed a single phrase for each Direction:

- East: Giving voice to innocence

- South: Applying will and persistence

- West: Opening the heart and soul

- North: Connecting to stability and foundation

- Above: Celebrating the wisdom

- Below: Grounding in the mystery

As the second part of this process, I began repeating the phrases and went into a light trance. An animal appeared to me almost immediately. Later, I did a shamanic journey to that animal to ask permission and to talk with it. The third part of the process was to dance the animal in the power dance journey found earlier in this book.

What emerged from the process were the totems used for the rituals found in this book. They are part of working circles, and if you choose to work with them, you will add your energy to the work that has been done before. You will experience magic and power as you work energetically with these totems. You may never know the names of the people working with them, but your work will add to the collected wisdom and knowledge found on all the planes of existence.

For East, I found Robin willing to sing with me and ready to give voice in my circle. For South, I found that Cheetah, as a creature of determination and speed, wanted to work within my circle. For West, I found that Otter, a creature of both fresh and salt water, wanted to play and lead me to ecstasy. For North, I found that Bear, as a creature of earth, wanted to show me the power of stability and place. For Above, I discovered that Eagle wanted to fly in celebration of wisdom. For Below, I found that Snake wanted to show me the mysteries of transformation and change.

I then wrote quarter calls and a circle cast that acknowledged the energies of these totems. I continue to work with them and honor their gifts to me. As with most things in spiritual life, it is all about the practice. Continuing to learn and understand the totems is done by visiting them regularly in trance, by thanking them and honoring them in our daily life, and by continuing our awareness of them. There is nothing more magical than, as numerous teachers before me have said, "just doing the work." The magic is in the practice. The practice is in the magic.

Steps in Finding and Working
with Your Circle Totems

This process will take some time, since each direction is a separate set of journeys and meditations. Take your time and enjoy it; while these are deep and wise journeys, the spiritual process is aimed at exploring all aspects of ourselves, including play, humor, and fun.

- Spend some time working with the directions and the elements. Write down some aspects of those directions that you would like to explore on a regular basis, i.e., where you would like to go deeper.

- Create a phrase from those thoughts for each of the directions.

- In a sacred space, go into a light trance and find a totem for each direction.

- Take a shamanic journey to the totem animals and ask for permission and wisdom.

- Dance each animal in a power animal dance.

Be sure to record the wisdom of your journeys, and begin to incorporate your shamanic wisdom into your Wiccan Book of Shadows. This further entwines the two practices into your spiritual life. You will find that each totem will teach you many things, and this will deepen your work with the Lord and Lady as well. You will feel even more a part of the interconnected Universe.

The next section contains ritual using our totems to explore many of the things touched upon earlier in the book. The rituals are both a place to learn and a place to celebrate. Take your time with them, repeating them as you need. Rituals can be as simple or as fancy as you like. These rituals are written for one person, but can easily be adapted for a group. The format of the rituals will be the same, providing you with a framework to write your own rituals as you deepen your practice. The ritual framework is written below. One of the values of repeating the same altar devotions, circle castings, and quarter calls is that each time they are used, the power behind the words are strengthened and empowered. As always with my written rituals, you are welcome to adapt them to suit your own special circumstances and needs.

Ritual Framework for the Shamanic Witch

I usually drum during parts of the ritual, or use drums and rattles to hail the powers when the quarters are called and when the God and Goddess are called. Infuse ceremonial aspects and drumming into this ritual to make it personal and deeply powerful. As before:

Create Sacred Space: This is the part where all of the ordinary reality needs are taken care of. Cleaning the space, and providing safety and privacy is an important part of creating sacred space. This is where you can intentionally set up the altar and set the tone for the work you are about to do.

Altar Devotion: Light the incense, and move your hand into the smoke so that it moves over your body, and say, "I breathe in the breath of the Goddess. I cast all negativity to the winds of change that I may be cleansed in Her intuition."

Light the candle, and move your hand over the flame so that the heat moves toward your body, and say, "I feel the passion of the Goddess. I cast all negativity to the fires of change that I may be cleansed in her vitality."

Dip your hands in the water, and sprinkle it over you, and say, "I bathe in the heart of the Goddess. I cast all negativity into the well of change that I maybe cleansed by Her love."

Take some of the salt, and sprinkle it over you, and say, "I stand in presence of the Goddess. I cast all negativity into the earth that I may be cleansed in her dark silence."

Move your hand deosil over all the elements, and say, "By air, fire, water, earth and by intuition, passion, love, and dark silence, I am a vessel of the Goddess."

Cleanse the Circle: Add salt to the chalice, and move widdershins around the circle, chanting, "By salt and water, this circle is cleansed."

Purify the Circle: Light incense, and move widdershins around the circle, chanting, "By air and fire, this circle is cleansed."

Cast the Circle: Begin in the North and, with athame pointed to the ground, walk around the circle with these words. If you finish before you reach the North, walk in silence.

> I conjure now the powers of dark and light
> Encircle us with love, clear and bright.
> Move us into time-no-time

Between the worlds of place-no-place
Where magick is born and wonder happens.

Beginning at the North, walk deosil and hold the athame at shoulder length, and chant:

By the power of my hand, I cast the magick circle round
To create a shield, shining bright, to protect,
defend, and guard us.
From North, South, East, and West,
we call blessings to this place.

By roots and rocks we call below
To the beauty of the earth
Into our circle flow.
By the stars in the darkened sky,
We call magick, come, into our circle fly.

Starting at the North, hold the athame in the air with one hand and the other hand to the ground, and say:

Hail to the powers of the starry Heavens
Surround and protect us this dark sacred night
Keep us safe 'till the dawn of the bright blessed day.
Open our souls to see beyond the Veil
To greet the ancestors of blood and bone, heart
and soul.

Stand at the North, holding the athame high in one hand and the other hand to the ground. Stomp your foot, and chant:

By the full moon and by sweet earth, this circle
is sealed.

We are between the worlds.

Blessed be!

Center and Ground: In silence, find your connection to Mother Earth and bring that energy into your body. When that energy begins to move and dance with yours, move your awareness out of the crown of your head, and find connection with the Universe. Take one long, deep breath from the top of your head, to the tips of your fingers, to the tips of your toes. Know that you are centered and grounded.

Call the Quarters:

North:

> By the powers of strength and silence,
> I call you, Bear, guardian of rich earth.
> Come foundation, come stability, come Gnome
> Bring your protection, mighty North.
> Hail and welcome.

East:

> By the powers of mind and intuition,
> I call you, Robin, creature of song.
> Come innocence, come joy, come Sylph
> Bring your brightness, sweet East.
> Hail and welcome.

South:

> By the powers of purpose and intention,
> I call you, Cheetah, moving with determination.

Come will, come persistence, come Salamander.

Bring your power, mighty South.

Hail and welcome.

West:

By the powers of healing and love,

I call you, Otter, playing in the sea.

Come heart, come feeling, come

Undines Bring your soul, loving West.

Center:

By the powers of union and connection,

I call you, Eagle, farseeing and wise

Fly from Above and into the Center fly;

I call you, Snake, changing and wise,

Move from Below and into the Center come.

Wisdom and mystery, rise and flow

Meet in the center with magic and love.

Hail and welcome.

Call to the Goddess or God:

Call the Goddess:

Lady of the Moon, lady

Of our hearts, be here in our circle.

Bring love, peace

And joy to our rite.

Hail and welcome.

Call the God:

> Lord of the Hunt, wise
> And mighty Warrior.
> Be here in our circle.
> Bring courage, will,
> And power to our circle.
> Hail and welcome.

Farewell to the Goddess or God:

Statement of Ritual Intent: State what it is that you intend to do.

- Go to your place in nature.

- Call your power animal(s) to you.

- State your intention three times.

- Journey.

- When the drum signals to return, follow the same pathway back to the starting point.

Raise the Cone of Power: This is where you chant or sing words of power stemming from your work. With your intention and will you send this energy into the Universe to enliven your goal.

Farewell to the God:

> Farewell Mighty Hunter.
> Go with our thanks and our blessings
> Hail and farewell.

Farewell to the Goddess:

> Loving Lady of the Moon
> Go with our thanks and our blessings
> Half and farewell.

Dismiss the Quarters:

Center:

> Fare thee well, Eagle and Snake
> Above and Below
> In perfect trust from us go.
> Hail and farewell.

West:

> Fare thee well, magical West
> Otter and Undines
> In perfect trust from us go.
> Hail and farewell.

South:

> Fare thee well, passionate South
> Cheetah and Salamanders
> In perfect trust from us go.
> Hail and farewell.

East:

> Fare thee well, knowing East
> Robin and Sylphs
> In perfect trust from us go.
> Hail and farewell.

North:

> Fare thee well, silent North
>
> Bear and Gnomes
>
> In perfect trust from us go.
>
> Hail and farewell.

Take up the Circle: With your athame pointed to the ground, move widdershins around the circle, and as you do, imagine the circle moving back into the knife. When you reach the North, place the tip of the blade downward and send the energy back into Mother Earth, with thanks.

Ritual of Warding and Protection

I have never liked sounding overly paranoid about safety and magical protection because I truly believe that the Universe is an abundant and loving place. But the fact of the matter is that the Goddess and God call us to be smart about our lives, and this includes commonsense approaches to safety. It is not a good idea to let yourself be vulnerable to thievery or attack. Know the area in which you live, know what it is to be safe in that area, and then take the proper precautions.

Taking the proper and sensible precautions in sacred space is also a good idea. You can protect your home, property, and your own physical safety by setting wards in the corners of your property. You choose totems or deities who are willing to do this work for you, to serve as guardians. I recommend choosing totems that you do not normally work with; for example, ones that could not be predicted. Then tell no one, or only a trusted few—I recommend as few as possible as part of the "to keep silent" principle of magick. I have written mine in my Book of Shadows, a book that is not shared with others. As you do this, you will have to "renew" the warding on a regular basis. That means you will need to go to those guardians and thank them for their service, and ask them if they would like to continue the work. I do this as part of preparation for one of the harvest Sabbats. I also make sure that I thank them on a regular basis. I make offerings to the Middle World counterparts as an expression of gratitude and thanksgiving.

There are a couple of differences in this ritual, since the magic is staying in place for an opened-ended period of time. At the end of the ritual, the circle is not taken up, but opened deosil. The circle is open, but you continue to be surrounded by the magic and power of the circle.

Create Sacred Space: Journey for the guardians whom you wish to have serve as protectors of your space. Find ones for North, East, South, West, Above, and Below. Be sure to ask their permission and get their consent before doing the ritual. Thank them, and make offerings to them and their Middle World counterparts.

Set up your ritual space, and before beginning the ritual walk widdershins completely around your property and extend your awareness slightly beyond the borders. If you feel comfortable doing this where people can see you, rattle around the area as you walk. Then walk deosil around the property with your awareness extended slightly beyond the borders. When I lived in a townhouse, I walked completely around the rows of houses in the back and around the parking lot in the front. If you feel comfortable, drum as you walk deosil. Otherwise, in both walks chant or sing your power song for each widdershins time around your space. This ritual can be done whether you own the property or not. The important thing is that it is where you reside, it is your home, and you deserve to be safe from harm wherever you are!

Enter your ritual space and begin the ritual. In the warding part of the ritual, you may want to substitute the qualities of the guardian you have chosen for each direction. You may also wish to choose specific deities to call into the circle as God and Goddess. As always with my rituals, please change them to suit your particular needs.

Altar Devotion: Light the incense, and move your hand into the smoke so that it moves over your body, and say, "I breathe in the breath of the Goddess. I cast all negativity to the winds of change that I may be cleansed in Her intuition."

Light the candle, and move your hand over the flame so that the heat moves toward your body, and say, "I feel the passion of the Goddess. I cast all negativity to the fires of change that I may be cleansed in Her vitality."

Dip your hands in the water and sprinkle it over you, and say, "I bathe in the heart of the Goddess. I cast all negativity into the well of change that I maybe cleansed by Her love."

Take some of the salt and sprinkle it over you, and say, "I stand in presence of the Goddess. I cast all negativity into the earth that I may be cleansed in Her dark silence."

Move your hand deosil over all the elements, and say, "By air, fire, water, earth and by intuition, passion, love, and dark silence, I am a vessel of the Goddess."

Cleanse the Circle: Add salt to the chalice, and move widdershins around the circle, chanting, "By salt and water, this circle is cleansed."

Purify the Circle: Light incense, and move widdershins around the circle, chanting, "By air and fire, this circle is cleansed."

Cast the Circle: Begin in the North, and with athame pointed to the ground, walk around the circle with these words. If you finish before you reach the North, walk in silence.

> I conjure now the powers of dark and light
> Encircle us with love, clear and bright.
> Move us into time-no-time
> Between the worlds of place-no-place
> Where magick is born and wonder happens.

Beginning at the North, walk deosil and hold the athame at shoulder-length, and chant:

> By the power of my hand, I cast the magick circle round
> To create a shield, shining bright, to protect,
> defend, and guard us.
> From North, South, East, and West,
> we call blessings to this place.
>
> By roots and rocks we call below
> To the beauty of the earth
> Into our circle flow.

By the stars in the darkened sky,
We call magick, come, into our circle fly.

Starting at the North, hold the athame in the air with one hand and the other hand to the ground, and say:

Hail to the powers of the starry Heavens
Surround and protect us this dark sacred night
Keep us safe 'till the dawn of the bright blessed day.
Open our souls to see beyond the Veil
To greet the ancestors of blood and bone, heart
and soul.

Stand at the North, holding the athame high in one hand and the other hand to the ground. Stomp your foot, and chant:

By the full moon and by sweet earth, this circle
is sealed.
We are between the worlds.
Blessed be!

Center and Ground: In silence, find your connection to Mother Earth and bring that energy into your body. When that energy begins to move and dance with yours, move your awareness out of the crown of your head, and find connection with the Universe. Take one long, deep breath from the top of your head, to the tips of your fingers, to the tips of your toes. Know that you are centered and grounded.

Call the Quarters:

North:

By the powers of strength and silence,
I call you, Bear, guardian of rich earth.

Come foundation, come stability, come Gnome
Bring your protection, mighty North.
Hail and welcome.

East:

By the powers of mind and intuition,
I call you, Robin, creature of song.
Come innocence, come joy, come Sylph
Bring your brightness, sweet East.
Hail and welcome.

South:

By the powers of purpose and intention,
I call you, Cheetah, moving with determination.
Come will, come persistence, come Salamander
Bring your power, mighty South.
Hail and welcome.

West:

By the powers of healing and love,
I call you, Otter, playing in the sea.
Come heart, come feeling, come Undines
Bring your soul, loving West.

Center:

By the powers of union and connection,
I call you, Eagle, farseeing and wise.
Fly from Above and into the Center fly;
I call you, Snake, changing and wise,
Move from Below and into the Center come.

Wisdom and mystery, rise and flow

Meet in the Center with magic and love.

Hail and welcome.

Call to the Goddess or God:

Call the Goddess:

Lady of abundance and safety,

I call you to come, come to the circle.

Bring warmth, love, and protection,

Bring your wisdom, and bring your power.

Beloved Lady, hail and welcome.

Call the God:

Lord of the hunt, Consort of the Lady,

I call you to come, come to the circle.

Bring your wildness, your power, and strength,

Bring your might and bring your protection.

Lord of the Wild Ones, hail and welcome.

Statement of Ritual Intent: Today, I ask that these beings, [names], gathered here to serve as my guardians, to protect me and keep me from harm. I ask that they use their power and magic to keep all who mean ill away from me, my property, my loved ones, and my space. I ask this in perfect love and perfect trust.

The Warding: Begin in the North. Use your athame to direct the energy and power you are wielding.

Face North, and point your athame to the northern edge of your property, and say:

Hail powers of the North, of stability, firmness, and dark, deep, silent power. Greet this guardian of the North. This [name] agrees to be the power of the North in all its silence and might; to guard and protect those within this place, and keep all safe from harm. All who mean ill, keep them away from this place. So mote it be!

In a fluid motion, move your athame around the circle to the East. Point your athame to the eastern edge of your property, and say:

Hail powers of the East, of discernment, wisdom, intuition, and intelligence. Greet this guardian of the East. This [name] agrees to be the power of the East in all its discernment and intuition; to guard and protect those within this place, and keep all safe from harm. All who mean ill, keep them away from this place. So mote it be!

In a fluid motion, move your athame around the circle to the South. Point your athame to the southern edge of your property, and say:

Hail powers of the South, of will, effectiveness, transformation, and passion. Greet this guardian of the South. This [name] agrees to be the power of the South in all its will, energy, and power; to guard and protect those within this place, and keep all safe from harm. All who mean ill, keep them away from this place. So mote it be!

In a fluid motion, move your athame around the circle to the West. Point your athame to the western edge of your property, and say:

Hail powers of the West, of love, generosity, heart, emotion, and desire. Greet this guardian of the West. This [name] agrees to be the power of the South in all its healing, magic, and mystery; to guard and protect those within this place, and keep all safe from harm. All who mean ill, keep them away from this place. So mote it be!

In a fluid motion, move your athame around the circle to the North, completing it. Move your athame downward and visualize the circle encompassing the earth beneath your feet and floor. Stand in the center and point your athame below, and say:

Hail powers of Below, of roots, mud, ancestors, death, and beyond. Greet this guardian of Below. This [name] agrees to be the power of Below in all its death, roots, and ancestral wisdom; to guard and protect those within this place, and keep all safe from harm. All who mean ill, keep them away from this place. So mote it be!

In a fluid motion, move your athame above the circle, encompassing the air above your place. Stand in the center and point your athame above, and say:

Hail powers of Above, of celestial wisdom, teaching, and infinity. Greet this guardian of Above. This [name] agrees to be the power of Above in all its celestial beauty and infinite wisdom; to guard and protect those within this place, and keep all safe from harm. All who mean ill, keep them away from this place. So mote it be!

Stand in the center, and raise your arms and address all that are assembled as witnesses and guardians:

Hail powers of infinite wisdom, hail powers of strength, beauty, and purpose. Greet and accept these guardians as protectors of me, this space, and those beloved. Hold the safety of those dwelling here, and this place as sacred. Guard and protect all who come here in love and trust. We ask this magic for the good of all and the harm of none. In wisdom, love, and power, we ask blessings, protection, and love. Guard and protect us, hold us from harm and keep us in love. So mote it be!

With the words "So mote it be," raise a cone of power and send it into the Universe with a big "whoosh" for safety, protection, and guardianship.

Center by taking a deep breath, and ground by renewing your connection to the energy of Mother Earth.

Farewell to the God or Goddess:

Farewell to the God:

> Great Lord, mighty Hunter,
> Thank you for the great love you hold.
> Thank you for your strength and protection.
> Go with our thanks and our blessings,
> Hail and farewell.

Farewell to the Goddess:

> Loving Mother, gracious Goddess,
> Thank you for your wisdom and the protection
> of your presence,
> And the wonders that you bring to us
> Body and soul.

Go with our thanks and our blessings.
Hail and farewell.

Dismiss the Quarters:

Center:

Fare thee well, Eagle and Snake
Above and Below
In perfect trust from us go.
Hail and farewell.

West:

Fare thee well, magical West
Otter and Undines
In perfect trust from us go.
Hail and farewell.

South:

Fare thee well, passionate South
Cheetah and Salamanders
In perfect trust from us go.
Hail and farewell.

East:

Fare thee well, knowing East
Robin and Sylphs
In perfect trust from us go.
Hail and farewell.

North:

Fare thee well, silent North
Bear and Gnomes

In perfect trust from us go.

Hail and farewell.

Open the Circle: Move deosil around the circle, envisioning the power of the circle dissipating, but allowing the magic to linger. If you move away from this place, you will need to release the guardians from their service and take up the circle by going widdershins.

Celebrating My Body Divine: A Ritual to Celebrate and Bless my Embodiment

This ritual is a continuation of the embodiment work done with the mirrors. It takes the wisdom you have gained and puts in a ritual as celebration, and as a way to seal the work you have done. The work done in ordinary reality becomes real and alive on all the spiritual planes.

Create Sacred Space: Clean and beautify the space where you will hold this ritual. Also beautify yourself in ways that are special to you, including ritual baths, scents, special jewelry, and a light meal. If you intend to do this ritual skyclad, wear a beautiful, flowing robe. If you intend to be clothed, wear something special to you. For this ritual, you will need a large mirror, full-length if possible. You will also need consecration oil1, a chalice of water, and a little wine.

Altar Devotion: Light the incense, and move your hand into the smoke so that it moves over your body, and say, "I breathe in the breath of the Goddess. I cast all negativity to the winds of change that I may be cleansed in Her intuition."

Light the candle, and move your hand over the flame so that the heat moves toward your body, and say, "I feel the passion of the Goddess. I cast all negativity to the fires of change that I may be cleansed in Her vitality."

Dip your hands in the water and sprinkle it over you, and say, "I bathe in the heart of the Goddess. I cast all negativity into the well of change that I maybe cleansed by Her love."

Take some of the salt, and sprinkle it over you, and say, "I stand in presence of the Goddess. I cast all negativity into the earth that I may be cleansed in her dark silence."

Move your hand deosil over all the elements and say, "By air, fire, water, earth and by intuition, passion, love, and dark silence, I am a vessel of the Goddess."

Cleanse the Circle: Add salt to the chalice, and move widdershins around the circle, chanting, "By salt and water, this circle is cleansed."

Purify the Circle: Light incense, and move widdershins around the circle, chanting, "By air and fire, this circle is cleansed."

Cast the Circle: Begin in the North, and with athame pointed to the ground, walk around the circle with these words. If you finish before you reach the North, walk in silence.

I conjure now the powers of dark and light
Encircle us with love, clear and bright.
Move us into time-no-time
Between the worlds of place-no-place
Where magick is born and wonder happens.

Beginning at the North, walk deosil and hold the athame at shoulder-length, and chant:

By the power of my hand, I cast the magick circle round
To create a shield, shining bright, to protect, defend,
and guard us.
From North, South, East, and West, we call blessings to
this place.

By roots and rocks we call below,
To the beauty of the earth
Into our circle flow.
By the stars in the darkened sky,
We call magick, come, into our circle fly.

Starting at the North, hold the athame in the air with one hand and the other hand to the ground, and say:

Hail to the powers of the starry Heavens
Surround and protect us this dark sacred night
Keep us safe 'till the dawn of the bright blessed day.
Open our souls to see beyond the Veil
To greet the ancestors of blood and bone,
heart and soul.

Stand at the North, holding the athame high in one hand and the other hand to the ground. Stomp your foot, and chant:

> By the moon and by sweet earth, this circle is sealed.
> We are between the worlds.
> Blessed be!

Center and Ground: In silence, find your connection to Mother Earth and bring that energy into your body. When that energy begins to move and dance with yours, move your awareness out of the crown of your head, and find connection with the Universe. Take one long, deep breath from the top of your head, to the tips of your fingers, to the tips of your toes. Know that you are centered and grounded.

Call the Quarters:

North:

> By the powers of strength and silence
> I call you, Bear, guardian of rich earth.
> Come foundation, come stability, come Gnome
> Bring your protection, mighty North.
> Hail and welcome.

East:

> By the powers of mind and intuition,
> I call you, Robin, creature of song.
> Come innocence, come joy, come Sylph
> Bring your brightness, sweet East.
> Hail and welcome.

South:

> By the powers of purpose and intention,
> I call you, Cheetah, moving with determination.
> Come will, come persistence, come Salamander
> Bring your power, mighty South.
> Hail and welcome.

West:

> By the powers of healing and love,
> I call you, Otter, playing in the sea.
> Come heart, come feeling, come Undines
> Bring your soul, loving West.

Center:

> By the powers of union and connection,
> I call you, Eagle, farseeing and wise
> Fly from Above and into the Center fly;
> I call you, Snake, changing and wise,
> Move from Below and into the Center come.
> Wisdom and mystery, rise and flow
> Meet in the Center with magic and love.
> Hail and welcome.

Call to the Goddess or God:

Call the Goddess:

> Lady of beauty, Lady of song
> Sweet body of the earth
> In beauty and bounty, I call you.

Come to my circle and stay

Be witness and companion

Bring blessings and love.

Hail and welcome.

Call the God:

Lord of the hunt, Lord of the wild

Lover and beloved

In beauty and strength, I call you.

Come to my circle and stay

Be witness and companion

Bring power and understanding.

Hail and welcome.

Statement of Ritual Intent: I am here to bless, consecrate, and celebrate my body, the embodiment of the divine and sacred.

The Work: Stand before the mirror, skyclad if possible. Have the water, consecration oil, and wine within easy reach. (Please note that we are blessing various parts of our body, so feel free to change what I have written here to single out and celebrate what is appropriate for you!)

Take a deep breath, look into the mirror, and say, "In the presence of these assembled powers, I celebrate my body. Before earth, air, fire, and water, and in the loving presence of the Lord and Lady, I bless my body."

Hold the water up, and say, "With this water, I bless my body in love and trust, blessed be."

Hold the wine up, and say, "With this wine, I consecrate my sacred self, in love and trust, blessed be."

Hold the oil up, and say, "With this oil, I beautify the essence of my divinity in love and trust, blessed be."

Anoint the parts of your body that you wish to celebrate, starting with your feet and moving upward. Use water followed by wine followed by oil, and say words that mean something special to you. You can be spiritual, practical, funny, ironic and positive, but you must be personal and you must not be negative. You can acknowledge your struggles, but you must frame them in positive statements. The following are examples of statements you might make.

- Blessed are my feet. They keep me firm and steady on my path.

- Blessed are my ankles. They keep me strong and upright as I walk.

- Blessed are my knees. They keep me humble before the Lord and Lady, and straight and tall before all others.

- Blessed are my thighs. They are what they are.

- Blessed is my sex. It brings me pleasure and brings forth abundance.

- Blessed is my belly. It makes big laughs and nurtures me.

- Blessed are my hips. They help me swivel and turn.

- Blessed are my ribs. They are strong and hold my insides safe.

- Blessed are my breasts and chest. They keep my heart safe.

- Blessed are my hands. They create beauty and bring pleasure.

- Blessed are my elbows. They hold my head up when my neck is too tired.

- Blessed are my shoulders. They carry the weight of worry.

- Blessed is my throat. It controls my words and sounds.

- Blessed is my mouth. It says words of strength and sings songs of beauty.

- Blessed is my nose. It brings the perfume of pleasure, and the odor of warning.

- Blessed are my eyes. They see clear and bright.

- Blessed is my forehead. It houses and protects my brain.

- Blessed is my hair. It is soft and silky.

- Blessed is my crown. It connects me with the Universe.

Raise the Cone of Power: While this may seem silly, it is extraordinarily effective. Raise a cone of power by chanting:

> Blessed be me
> Blessed be me
> Blessed be me
> *Me, me, me, meeeeee* until the energy goes *whoosh*
> into the Universe!

Grounding and Centering: Renew your connection to the earth. Feel the firmness and stability of it as you breathe in the power of the earth.

Farewell to the God or Goddess:

Farewell to the God:

> Lord of the hunt, Lord of love
> Fare thee well.
> Thank you for the love and blessings.
> Hail and farewell.

Farewell to the Goddess:

> Lady of love, Lady of bounty
> Fare thee well.
> Thank you for the love and blessings.
> Hail and farewell.

Dismiss the Quarters:

Center:

> Fare thee well, Eagle and Snake
> Above and Below
> In perfect trust from us go.
> Hail and farewell.

West:

> Fare thee well, magical West
> Otter and Undines
> In perfect trust from us go.
> Hail and farewell.

South:

> Fare thee well, passionate South
> Cheetah and Salamanders
> In perfect trust from us go.
> Hail and farewell.

East:

> Fare thee well, knowing East
> Robin and Sylphs
> In perfect trust from us go.
> Hail and farewell.

North:

> Fare thee well, silent North
> Bear and Gnomes
> In perfect trust from us go.
> Hail and farewell

Take up the Circle: With your athame pointed to the ground, move widdershins around the circle, and as you do, imagine the circle moving back into the knife. When you reach the North, place the tip of the blade downward and send the energy back into Mother Earth, with thanks.

Ritual Consecration of Your Magical Tools

This ritual combines some of the skills discussed in the beginning of the book and places them within a ritual, creating both a shamanic and a Craft-oriented relationship to your magical tools. The basic tool kit of the Shamanic Witch contains a drum, a rattle, a wand, a Book of Shadows, an athame, a chalice, and a pentacle. Other tools can include rocks, gems, crystals, moon water, jewelry, cords, divination tools, and other things created to assist with magical work. Anything that connects to you and you only while working magic can be consecrated to you. I teach a lot and am in a clergy training tradition, and since I am not very rigid about the "only I can touch consecrated objects" rule, I sometimes have to cleanse and rededicate the tools in ritual.

You build a relationship with your magical tools, so there is preparation work to do before this ritual. Earlier in the book, I described gazing and contemplation meditations for drums and rattles, which can be done for any tool and should be done for the basic elemental tools of wand, athame, chalice, and pentacle.

Create Sacred Space: For each object you intend to consecrate within this ritual, do the meditation of attuning to the object, repeated as follows. These meditations can be done over a period of time and, do not necessarily have to happen right before the ritual.

Stand in the center of your space, holding your object near your heart. Take a deep breath, and feel your energy fill your body, from head to toe and to the tips of your fingers. Feel your energy move into the object, filling it with beauty and light. Take one long, deep breath and feel the object connect with you. Breathe your energy into the object.

Continue breathing in this manner, and cast your awareness down to your feet and send roots down into the earth. As your roots go downward, feel the energy of the Earth Mother meld into the roots. Find a place to loop your roots, down deep in the earth, and stabilize yourself there, firmly but flexibly. Through your roots, breathe up the energy of the Earth Mother into yourself, and feel it meld and dance with the energy inside of you. When you are filled with the energy of the Earth Mother, cast your awareness to the object in your hands, and breathe this melded energy into the object. Continue to breathe this combined energy into the object.

Continue breathing in this manner, and then cast your awareness to the crown of your head. Send your energy outward into the Universe, and feel the energy of the Universe reach out to you and embrace you. As you are embraced, feel this energy merge with the combined energy of you and the Earth Mother. Feel it move downward through your crown and into your body. Breathe in that energy and feel it meld together, a triplicity of beauty and delight. When that energy has filled you from head to toe and to the tips of your fingers, cast your awareness to your hands and the object there.

Breathe energy into that object. Keep breathing deeply so that you are connected to the object, and it is filled with the combined energy. When the connection is deep and strong, gently move your roots away from the anchoring spot and bring them gently back to your feet. Then, cast your awareness up into the Universe, where you are still being held, and gently move out of that embrace. Move the energy back into yourself. Stay connected to your object, and breathe deeply once so that your awareness is completely back into your space. Breathe again to fully open your eyes and awareness to your space.

You may want to assemble herbs and oils that have special meaning to you or that you use regularly. You create traditions and special signatures by consistently using similar herbal or oil combinations in your magical work. In this ritual, I will be using oils to anoint the tool.[3] Only a tiny amount is needed, so use no more than one or two drops of the oil combined in a carrier such as almond oil, jojoba oil, or olive oil. The following is a list of herbal and oil combinations and their purposes.

- Orange essential oil for a scented high note that is for cleansing, purification, and love

- Patchouli for grounding and connection with the earth below our feet

- Dragons blood for empowerment, energy, and protection

- Clary sage for wisdom, psychic awareness, and divination

Depending on the tool, you will either anoint it directly, or sprinkle the oil around it.

For this ritual, you will need a cauldron or bowl to serve as a cauldron of transformation. A cast iron Dutch oven works well for a cauldron. Place the cauldron or bowl in the center of your altar in front of your symbols for the Goddess and God.

As you set up your sacred space, you will be working at your altar and will need tools for each of the quarters: salt in the North; incense or a fan in the East; a candle in the South; water in the West; and, the anointing oil in the Center.

Altar Devotion: Light the incense, and move your hand into the smoke so that it moves over your body, and say, "I breathe in the breath of the Goddess. I cast all negativity to the winds of change that I may be cleansed in Her intuition."

Light the candle, and move your hand over the flame so that the heat moves toward your body, and say, "I feel the passion of the Goddess. I cast all negativity to the fires of change that I may be cleansed in Her vitality."

Dip your hands in the water and sprinkle it over you, and say, "I bathe in the heart of the Goddess. I cast all negativity into the well of change that I maybe cleansed by Her love."

Take some of the salt and sprinkle it over you, and say, "I stand in presence of the Goddess. I cast all negativity into the earth that I may be cleansed in her dark silence."

Move your hand deosil over all the elements, and say, "By air, fire, water, earth and by intuition, passion, love, and dark silence, I am a vessel of the Goddess."

Cleanse the Circle: Add salt to the chalice, and move widdershins around the circle, chanting, "By salt and water, this circle is cleansed."

Purify the Circle: Light incense, and move widdershins around the circle, chanting, "By air and fire, this circle is cleansed."

Cast the Circle: Begin in the North, and with athame pointed to the ground, walk around the circle with these words. If you finish before you reach the North, walk in silence.

I conjure now the powers of dark and light
Encircle us with love, clear and bright.
Move us into time-no-time
Between the worlds of place-no-place
Where magick is born and wonder happens.

Beginning at the North, walk deosil and hold the athame at shoulder-length, and chant:

By the power of my hand, I cast the
magick circle round
To create a shield, shining bright, to protect,
defend, and guard us.
From North, South, East and West,
we call blessings to this place.

By roots and rocks we call below
To the beauty of the earth
Into our circle flow.
By the stars in the darkened sky,
We call magick, come, into our circle fly.

Starting at the North, hold the athame in the air with one hand and the other hand to the ground, and say:

Hail to the powers of the starry Heavens
Surround and protect us this dark sacred night
Keep us safe 'till the dawn of the bright blessed day.
Open our souls to see beyond the Veil
To greet the ancestors of blood and bone,
heart and soul.

Stand at the North, holding the athame high with one hand and the other hand to the ground. Stomp your foot, and chant:

> By the moon and by sweet earth, this circle is sealed.
> We are between the worlds.
> Blessed be!

Center and Ground: In silence, find your connection to Mother Earth, and bring that energy into your body. When that energy begins to move and dance with yours, move your awareness out of the crown of your head, and find connection with the Universe. Take one long, deep breath from the top of your head, to the tips of your fingers, to the tips of your toes. Know that you are centered and grounded.

Call the Quarters:

North:

> By the powers of strength and silence,
> I call you, Bear, guardian of rich earth.
> Come foundation, come stability, come Gnome
> Bring your protection, mighty North.
> Hail and welcome.

East:

> By the powers of mind and intuition,
> I call you, Robin, creature of song.
> Come innocence, come joy, come Sylph
> Bring your brightness, sweet East.
> Hail and welcome.

South:

> By the powers of purpose and intention,
> I call you, Cheetah, moving with determination.
> Come will, come persistence, come Salamander
> Bring your power, mighty South.
> Hail and welcome.

West:

> By the powers of healing and love,
> I call you, Otter, playing in the sea.
> Come heart, come feeling, come Undines
> Bring your soul, loving West.

Center:

> By the powers of union and connection,
> I call you, Eagle, farseeing and wise
> Fly from Above and into the Center fly;
> I call you, Snake, changing and wise,
> Move from Below and into the Center come.
> Wisdom and mystery, rise and flow
> Meet in the Center with magic and love.
> Hail and welcome.

Call to the Goddess or God:

Call the Goddess:

> Lady of learning, joy, and desire
> I call you to come, come to the circle.
> Bring dedication, learning, and understanding

Bring your wisdom, and bring your power.

Beloved Lady, hail and welcome.

Call the God:

Lord of the hunt, Consort of the Lady,

I call you to come, come to the circle.

Bring your wildness, your power and strength

Bring your might and bring your support.

Lord of the Wild Ones, hail and welcome.

Statement of Ritual Intent: Place the tool that you wish to consecrate onto your altar. Hold your hands over it, and say, "I come here today to consecrate this tool [name it] as a magical companion to my work, to service to the Lady and the Lord."

Consecration: Hold your tool over the northern edge of your altar and sprinkle it with salt, while chanting, "By flesh and earth, you are cleansed and consecrated in Her solid earth."

Hold your tool over the eastern edge of your altar and move it through the incense smoke (or wave the fan over it), while chanting, "By knowledge and intuition, you are cleansed and consecrated in Her sweet breath."

Hold your tool over the southern edge of your altar and wave it near or through the candle flame, while chanting, "By will and passion, you are cleansed and consecrated in Her fiery heat."

Hold your tool over the western edge of your altar and sprinkle it with water, while chanting, "By heart and soul, you are cleansed and consecrated by the waters of Her womb."

Place your tool in the cauldron at the center of your altar and sprinkle it with the oil mixture, while chanting, "By mystery and magic, by wisdom and infinity, I cleanse and consecrate you by the love of Her bright spirit."

Chant your power song over the cauldron and then pull out the tool, and with a strong voice say, "In love, power, and mystery you are reborn. From everyday object to magick reborn."

Present it to the Lady and the Lord and say, "To serve Them in perfect love, trust, and power. So mote it be! So mote it be!" On the final "so mote it be," send a cone of power out with a whoosh to consecrate the tool. So mote it be!

Center by taking a deep breath, and ground by renewing your connection to the energy of Mother Earth.

Farewell to the Goddess or God:

Farwell to the Goddess:

> Loving Mother, gracious Goddess
> Thank you for your wisdom and the protection
> of your presence,
> And the wonders that you bring to us
> Body and soul.
> Go with our thanks and our blessings.
> Hail and farewell.

Farewell to the God:

> Great Lord, mighty Hunter,
> Thank you for the great love you hold

Thank you for your strength and protection.

Go with our thanks and our blessings.

Hail and farewell.

Dismiss the Quarters:

Center:

Fare thee well, Eagle and Snake

Above and Below

In perfect trust from us go.

Hail and farewell.

West:

Fare thee well, magical West

Otter and Undines

In perfect trust from us go.

Hail and farewell.

South:

Fare thee well, passionate South

Cheetah and Salamanders

In perfect trust from us go.

Hail and farewell.

East:

Fare thee well, knowing East

Robin and Sylphs

In perfect trust from us go.

Hail and farewell.

North:

> Fare thee well, silent North
> Bear and Gnomes
> In perfect trust from us go.
> Hail and farewell.

Take up the circle: Walk widdershins around the circle, pointing your athame down toward the earth. Visualize the circle being taken into your athame. At the North, point the knife downward and allow the energy to go back into Mother Earth.

Shamanic Journeying within the Circle of the Witch

The three of us gathered for this ritual, long-time friends and circle-siblings. We created the altar together, each bringing our magical tools for the directions and other objects that had meaning for our stated intentions. The altar evolved beautifully and magically. We talked about the work we were about to do, important soul-level work.

We cast the circle and called in the directions, each calling in what was needed for our work. We called in the Lady and the Lord, each of us naming our patron Gods. We settled down to journey on our intentions.

The drumming began with intensity, and I was pulled immediately into my journey. Onward I went, meeting people from my past and receiving the needed tokens and messages. Some people from fractured and dead relationships refused to speak to me, so I had to steal the tokens from them. Finally, I was before the Goddess in a beautiful place. I gave her the tokens from my life, and she took them and transformed them into a black cord. She moved her hands, and we were in ritual circle. She and the assembled spirits initiated me and placed the black cord around my waist. The work had been done in these realms, even if the course of study did not happen with your chosen teacher. —you did the work, and it was done. It is good. She kissed me on both cheeks, and said, "Take your place among the other elders of this spiritual path." She handed me my drum, and I took my place in circle and we drummed an incredible cone of power. Whoosh!

Doing shamanic journeywork within a cast circle, using the magical words that you have written or are part of your tradition, is extremely powerful. The cast circle contains the power and intensifies the work. It is magical, transforming, and incredibly moving. The time and the magic that you have invested in creating rituals and working them in sacred space is intensified and amplified within the circle and before assembled spirits.

I think working with totems, using the six directions of North, East, South, West, Below, and Above, along with opening the Center, makes this a shamanic practice. By calling Above and Below into the Center, you open a portal between the Upper World and the Lower World, meeting in the Middle World; the circle becomes a place where all the worlds touch. The phrase "between the worlds" takes on new meaning and new power.

The spirits of the Upper World, Lower World, and Middle World know and respect the circle and the traditions that have used them. Because of the respect and honor given to ritual in Wicca and Witchcraft, these spirit beings know they will be heard and they will be honored.

The way to understand the incredible power and magic found while journeying in the circle is to do the journeywork. By now you should know that I believe the best way to learn and grow is to do the work. The most important part of this kind of spiritual life is practice. In your practice, you live out the values and magic that you espouse with your mouth and your mind. Your body is engaged, and melds with your mind and your spirit. The way to experience the dance of the ecstatic witch is to get up and dance. You can begin by tapping your foot to the heartbeat of the drum, but you also need to open your heart and soul and let the beating of the drum fill your body. Your blood and heart have the rhythm already—you just have to let it move you and fill you. Move. Practice. Dance the dance of ecstasy.

The following are some suggestions for shamanic journeying within a wiccan circle. Any journey suggested in this book or that you encounter in other books can be done within the circle. You will find your understanding in these journeys, merged with the magical energies with which you work will become deeper and incredibly rich.

- Journey to each of the elemental spirits: Sylphs of air, Salamanders of fire, Undines of water, and Gnomes of earth

- Journey to the ancient guardians of the directions

- Journey to individual Gods and Goddesses

- Journey to the spirit of the Sabbats: Yule, Imbolc, Ostara, Beltane, Midsummer, Lammas, Mabon, and Samhain

- Journey to the individual deities associated with the Sabbats

- Journey to the Moon Goddess(es) and each of Her phases

- Journey to the spirit of the individual Esbats

- Journey to the spirits of the Season

- Journey to the spirit guardians of your magical tools

- Journey on emotions such as love, grief, happiness, etc.

- Journey on your individual needs and desires

- Journey on what puzzles you, what grieves you, and what
  delights you

Ritual for the Journeywork Practice
of the Shamanic Witch

Create Sacred Space: Clean and consecrate your space. Hang decorations and create an altar that symbolizes the journey you are about to take. Take ritual baths and dress in ceremonial clothes as you find appropriate. Gather the tools and objects you need for the ritual and journey. If you are not comfortable drumming and journeying at the same time, using a drumming CD is extremely effective within the circle.

Altar Devotion: Light the incense, and move your hand into the smoke so that it moves over your body, and say, "I breathe in the breath of the Goddess. I cast all negativity to the winds of change that I may be cleansed in Her intuition."

Light the candle, and move your hand over the flame so that the heat moves toward your body, and say, "I feel the passion of the Goddess. I cast all negativity to the fires of change that I may be cleansed in Her vitality."

Dip your hands in the water and sprinkle it over you, and say, "I bathe in the heart of the Goddess. I cast all negativity into the well of change that I maybe cleansed by Her love."

Take some of the salt and sprinkle it over you, and say, "I stand in presence of the Goddess. I cast all negativity into the earth that I may be cleansed in Her dark silence."

Move your hand deosil over all the elements, and say, "By air, fire, water, earth and by intuition, passion, love, and dark silence, I am a vessel of the Goddess."

Cleanse the Circle: Add salt to the chalice, and move widdershins around the circle, chanting, "By salt and water, this circle is cleansed."

Purify the Circle: Light incense, and move widdershins around the circle, chanting, "By air and fire, this circle is cleansed."

Cast the Circle: Begin in the North, and with athame pointed to the ground, walk around the circle with these words. If you finish before you reach the North, walk in silence.

> I conjure now the powers of dark and light
> Encircle us with love, clear and bright.
> Move us into time-no-time

Between the worlds of place-no-place

Where magick is born and wonder happens.

Beginning at the North, walk deosil and hold the athame at shoulder length, and chant:

By the power of my hand, I cast the magick circle round

To create a shield, shining bright, to protect, defend,

and guard us.

From North, South, East, and West, we call blessings to

this place.

By roots and rocks we call below

To the beauty of the earth

Into our circle flow.

By the stars in the darkened sky,

We call magick, come, into our circle, fly.

Starting at the North, hold the athame in the air in one hand and the other hand to the ground, and say:

Hail to the powers of the starry Heavens

Surround and protect us this dark sacred night

Keep us safe 'till the dawn of the bright blessed day.

Open our souls to see beyond the Veil

To greet the ancestors of blood and bone,

heart and soul.

Stand at the North, holding the athame high in one hand and the other hand to the ground. Stomp your foot, and chant:

By the full moon and by sweet earth, this circle

is sealed.

We are between the worlds.
Blessed be!

Center and Ground: In silence, find your connection to Mother
Earth and bring that energy into your body. When that energy begins to move and dance with yours, move your awareness out of
the crown of your head, and find connection with the Universe.
Take one long, deep breath from the top of your head, to the tips
of your fingers, to the tips of your toes. Know that you are centered
and grounded.

Call the Quarters: Drum while calling the quarters; or, drum to
hail the powers of the North, ring a bell to hail the powers of the
East, shake a rattle to hail the powers of the South, and shake a
rainstick to hail the powers of the West. Use silence to hail the powers
of Above and Below.

North:

> By the powers of strength and silence,
> I call you, Bear, guardian of rich earth.
> Come foundation, come stability, come Gnome
> Bring your protection, mighty North.
> Hail and welcome.

East:

> By the powers of mind and intuition,
> I call you, Robin, creature of song.
> Come innocence, come joy, come Sylph
> Bring your brightness, sweet East.
> Hail and welcome.

South:

> By the powers of purpose and intention,
>
> I call you, Cheetah, moving with determination.
>
> Come will, come persistence, come Salamander
>
> Bring your power, mighty South.
>
> Hail and welcome.

West:

> By the powers of healing and love,
>
> I call you, Otter, playing in the sea.
>
> Come heart, come feeling, come Undines
>
> Bring your soul, loving West.

Center:

> By the powers of union and connection,
>
> I call you, Eagle, farseeing and wise
>
> Fly from Above and into the Center fly;
>
> I call you, Snake, changing and wise,
>
> Move from Below and into the Center come.
>
> Wisdom and mystery, rise and flow
>
> Meet in the Center with magic and love.
>
> Hail and welcome.

Call to the Goddess or God appropriate to your journey:

Statement of Ritual Intent: State what it is that you intend to do.

- Go to your place in nature.

- Call your power animal(s) to you.

- State your intention three times.

- Journey.

- When the drum signals to return, follow the same pathway back to the starting point.

Raise the Cone of Power: This is where you chant or sing words of power stemming from your work. With your intention and will you send this energy into the Universe to enliven your goal.

Farewell to the Goddess or God:

Farewell to the Goddess:

> Loving Lady of the Moon
> Go with our thanks and our blessings
> Half and farewell.

Farewell to the God:

> Farewell Mighty Hunter.
> Go with our thanks and our blessings
> Hail and farewell.

Dismiss the Quarters:

Center:

> Fare thee well, Eagle and Snake,
> Above and Below
> In perfect trust from us go.
> Hail and farewell.

West:

> Fare thee well, magical West,
>
> Otter and Undines
>
> In perfect trust from us go.
>
> Hail and farewell.

South:

> Fare thee well, passionate South,
>
> Cheetah and Salamanders
>
> In perfect trust from us go.
>
> Hail and farewell.

East:

> Fare thee well, knowing East,
>
> Robin and Sylphs
>
> In perfect trust from us go.
>
> Hail and farewell.

North:

> Fare thee well, silent North,
>
> Bear and Gnomes
>
> In perfect trust from us go.
>
> Hail and farewell.

Take up the Circle: With your athame pointed to the ground, move widdershins around the circle, and as you do, imagine the circle moving back into the knife. When you reach the North, place the tip of the blade downward and send the energy back into Mother Earth, with thanks.

You will find that journeying within a cast circle will intensify the work you are doing. Moreover, as you progress and explore shamanic healing and soul healing, you will learn that the circle provides protection and safety as well. It is an act of magic, an act of the witch, to combine these skills in this way. We step into the magic with skill and intention, and create transformation. We become the mystery because we are Shamanic Witches.

CONCLUSION AND INITIATION:
THE NEVERENDING CIRCLE

There is no real conclusion to the path of the Shamanic Witch, for even death takes us only to a different and new adventure. The dance of the Witch-Shaman integrates the journeywork and services of the shaman with the magical energy work of the witch. Both are healing paths, and both the witch and the shaman walk between the worlds in service of the sacred world. Both know that we are all connected and that we all create change when we dance in the web of life. Vibrant power is gained through deep experiences found in the heart of the wild and the Divine. Magic happens.

Wicca and Witchcraft are mystery religions. Ecstasy and magic occur when the Witch-Shaman lives fully as an embodied sacred being; understanding flaws and mistakes, and giving thanks for the energy that flows in and out of life. Generosity, power, forgiveness, thanksgiving, healing, joy, grief, love, and sorrow are all part of the experiences of those who walk and dance between the worlds. All of this is achieved by simply doing the work. It is an act of love, an act of boldness, an act of power, and an act of trust to cast a circle and journey through all the worlds.

It is a calling to be and to know. So what of initiation? How do I know I have the right to call myself a Shamanic Witch, you ask. The knowing comes after the work is done and the realization that it is all about the practice. That perfection is the process of going through the work.

Hear now the call of the Dancing Drum

Played by the hands of all the Gods.

Come dance with me and be.

Know in your body

Know in your soul

What it is to be.

Feel it in your feet as you dance my creatures

Dance your sorrow

Dance your joy.

Feel it in your heart as you meld with Me

Be as One with All-That-Is

You are Goddess

You are God.

Hear it in your voice as you sing your song

Sing of beauty, sing of ugliness

Sing of grief, sing of joy

Sing the Goddess and sing the God.

Open your arms and feel me there,

Open your heart and know my heartbeat

Open your soul and know my mystery.

Know that you are the knowing

You are the magic

You are the power.

You are the heartbeat

You are the Drum.

GLOSSARY

A

Alpha: The level of a hypnotic state where awareness is heightened. Daydreaming is an example of an alpha state.

Aspecting: In the practice of Wicca and Witchcraft, a skill and act when a facet of the Divine is channeled by the priest or priestess in order to understand a portion or characteristic of that Divine Being's persona. For instance, if a woman wanted to understand courage and independence better, she might aspect Artemis, Goddess of the hunt, in her aspect as Maiden and Huntress.

Axis Mundi: Also known as the World Tree, a center post, tree, or spear that pierces or goes through all the worlds of the material and spirit. Seen as a unifying symbol connecting the physical and the spirit worlds.

B

Beta: The awake and aware state of a human being, fully conscious and aware of surroundings and occurrences.

Book of Shadows: A record of a witch's magical work, typically a compilation of rituals, spells, and other magical work.

C

Ceremony: One of the many words for the act of honoring the relationship between human life and the spiritual world. In this book, it is meant to distinguish practices between a wiccan ritual and a shamanic practitioner's ritual.

Channeling: The act of receiving wisdom from a disincarnate being, whether dead or never living, and speaking or writing it for the benefit of other people. Mediums channel information from the beloved dead in the Spiritualist religion, while other people serve as long-term channels for an entity. The Seth Books by Jane Roberts are examples of channeling the wisdom of an entity. Channeling comes in many forms; see also *aspecting, drawing down, drawing up,* and *possession.*

Circle cast: In wiccan and Witchcraft tradition, the act of creating an energy line around ritual space for protection, privacy, and to move between the worlds of the material and spirit.

Clairaudience: In meditation, perceiving events in a meditative state through the sense of hearing. In the larger psychic sense, clairaudience is the ability to receive information and wisdom through hearing, whether in trance or in an ordinary state of awareness.

Clairsentience: In meditation, perceiving events in a meditative state through the tactile senses of feeling and smelling. In the larger psychic sense, clairsentience is the ability to receive information and wisdom through the feeling senses.

Clairvoyance: In meditation, perceiving events in a meditative state through the visual senses. In the larger psychic sense, clairvoyance is the ability to receive wisdom and information through the visual senses.

Consecration: In wiccan and Witchcraft traditions, the ritual act of blessing an object to the exclusive use of a witch, or a ritual to anoint, vow, and dedicate one's life to a spiritual path or to a deity.

D

Dance: In meditation and ritual, dance is used as an expression of devotion; it is also a shamanic act of union with the Divine or with the sacred beings of other planes. Dance can also be used as a meditation to gain wisdom and understanding of the life of the dancer and the dancer's relationship with the Divine; it can even be used as a form of prayer. In a magical and spell-casting sense, dance is used in a variety of ways to gain understanding of body memories, to raise energy, to heal, and to express devotion to the Gods.

Delta: The deepest and most profound state of trance, sleep, or somnambulism; those hypnotized are highly suggestible in this state.

Deosil: Moving clockwise or sunwise around the circle in wiccan and Witchcraft rituals.

Drawing down: In wiccan and Witchcraft traditions, the act of bringing the Goddess or God into the priestess or priest (respectively) for divination, or to ask wisdom of the deity. The priestess or priest is usually in a state of trance. Drawing down the moon is a full or waxing moon ceremony to receive the wisdom of the Full Moon Goddess.

Drawing Up: In wiccan and Witchcraft traditions, the act of drawing up the energy of Mother Earth into the priestess, usually for access to the wisdom of the earth. Not as commonly practiced as drawing down.

E

Ecstasy: In shamanic terms, the state of trance where the practitioner has moved out of their body and communes with the spirit worlds; the practitioner loses a sense of self as alone and isolated, and merges into a greater sense of universal love and connection.

Embodiment: The ability to live as a physical being, in acceptance and honor of one's own physical self, while at the same time knowing and acknowledging that a human being is an integrated whole of body, emotion, thought, experience, and soul.

Enhancement: A term coined by Judy Harrow, used to describe the lightest form of aspecting, where the priestess or priest feels a heightened sense of awareness but is still aware of their surroundings and events.

Esbat: In many and even most wiccan and Witchcraft terms, Esbat is a full moon celebration; in some traditions, an Esbat is any ritual celebrating the moon at any phase.

G

Gasso: The posture of prayer, with both palms together, held at the heart.

Grounding: The meditative act of connecting to the energies of Mother Earth; akin to drawing up.

Guardians: In wiccan and Witchcraft traditions, spiritual beings inhabiting other dimensions called into the ritual circle for protection and to witness the ritual.

I

Immanence: The term used to describe the sacred within each being. "You are God, you are Goddess," is often a greeting that acknowledges the divinity within a person.

Inspiration: The second level of aspecting as described by Judy Harrow, where the priestess or priest feels the presence of the Divine but is still aware and in control of their own actions.

Integration: The third level of aspecting as described by Judy Harrow, where the priestess or priest actually speaks as Goddess or God. This stage is often considered the stage of true aspecting.

Intention: In shamanic and ritual terms, the statement of what the ritual, meditation, or journey is going to do. The statement of intention helps direct the energy and attention of the practitioner and the entities assisting and guiding the witch or shaman.

Invocation: In wiccan and Witchcraft traditions, the act of calling in deities and spiritual energies directly into the priest or priestess for the purpose of divination or to gain further understanding or wisdom. It is also the term for the words used to call in the various energies of the quarters and the deities.

Invoking: See *invocation*.

J

Journey: In shamanic practice, the term for meditation where the practitioner goes into trance and walks in the spirit worlds.

L

Lower World: The spirit world located below the earth, which is a place of healing and of instinctual energies; the location and home of power animals and allies. Shamans travel there to gain insight, power, and information on healing, family, and the body.

M

Melding: Merging in meditation or ritual with disincarnate energies such as the deities, power animals, and guides.

Middle World: The material world and the plane of existence where the earth is found. Within the Middle World are the hidden worlds of devas and other such beings.

Mirror: A reflective surface, and also a magical tool to help the shamanic and magical practitioner access their own inner wisdom and inner selves.

N

Neo Shamanism: A term coined by Michael Harner and other modern practitioners to describe the shamanic practices of non-indigenous peoples, i.e., those inhabiting developed countries who no longer have a tradition of village life or village wise folk.

Nonordinary reality: A Neoshamanic term to describe the realities found on the spiritual planes of existence, most commonly referred to as the Lower World and the Upper World; also used to describe the ecstatic meditative trance journey.

O

Ordinary reality: A Neoshamanic term used to describe the reality experienced in the material world when not in meditation.

Ordinary States of Consciousness (OSS): A Neoshamanic term used to describe the trance state (or lack thereof) of people in an awake and aware state.

P

Possession: The meditative and aspecting state where the entity inhabits the person and the person then has an awareness of what is going on. Their descriptions include analogies to going to sleep and waking up afterward.

Power: The word "power" has a bad reputation. In a shamanic sense, power is gained through walking between the worlds and gaining information to be used in service to others. Walkers who use power in service of self and to control others are considered sorcerers.

Power animals: In a shamanic sense, spirit beings in the shape of animals who access the magical spirit of that animal, and who work with the shamanic practitioner. Most people have one or two guardian animals who are with them their entire lives, and then other animals who may assist them for specific tasks or for times of shorter durations.

Power objects: For the shamanic practitioner, various tools and things that are imbued with special properties that assist the practitioner in their work. These can include wands, herbs, stones, runes, cards, chalices, and any object that actually or symbolically aids the practitioners.

Power song: The voice and the song are strong tools and skills for the shamanic practitioner. Each person has a special soul song that expresses their soul. This song aids the practitioner as they seek information and power. There are other songs as well that help the practitioner develop special skills and abilities, so a practitioner may have a special song for cleansing and another for soul healing, and still another for healing the body.

R

Ritual: In wiccan and Witchcraft traditions, ritual is the central practice and celebration of connection to the earth and the Sacred. In these traditions, there are particular structures and customs associated with rituals.

S

Sabbat: In wiccan and Witchcraft traditions as well as other pagan and shamanic traditions, these are the sun or seasonal holidays. In modern practice, the eight Sabbats follow the Wheel of the Year, which has its roots in a variety of Celtic cultures, and are known as Yule, Imbolc, Ostara, Beltane, Midsummer, Lammas, Mabon, and Samhain. Spellings and names will vary.

Shaman: According to scholar Mircea Eliade, "the technicians of ecstasy," are those who are able to walk between the worlds, seeking knowledge, information, and power in service to their communities. It also refers to the skill set needed to complete these tasks. In modern usage, "shaman" is used for those born and living in indigenous cultures, while "shamanic practitioner" or other similar term is used for those who were born in the developed countries and now practice one of the variations of shamanic meditation and ceremony.

Shamanic States of Consciousness (SSC): The term used to describe the meditative state for those practicing shamanic journeying.

T

Teachers: In shamanic terms, the spirit allies inhabiting the Upper World who most often appear in human forms as Goddesses, heroes, and revered ancestors. Their purpose is to teach.

Theta: A deep trance state with a heightened sense of creativity.

Totem: An animal spirit that works with a person or a group of people such as a clan, family, or religious tradition. Sometimes the definition overlaps with power animals and allies. The totem holds symbolic meaning, as well as an interactive, personal meaning.

Trance: A deep state of hypnotism or meditation; in a shamanic sense, the practitioner maintains a strong control over the ability to be in trance and to direct the actions occurring within the hypnotic state.

Transcendence: In the spiritual sense, referring to the sacred found outside of humans and temporal creatures as eternal and nonphysical.

U

Upper World: The world of Spirit found above our heads. It is perceived as lighter and more ethereal than the Middle World and the Lower World. It is where the teachers and celestial beings are found.

V

Visualization: A form of meditation, most often guided, where the seeker is led through a scenario to seek wisdom and guidance.

W

Warding: The act through ritual or other magical work of creating protections around space and people.

Widdershins: Moving counter-clockwise or moon-wise around a circle. Considered a releasing or banishing energy.

NOTES

Chapter 1

1. Scott, Gini Ghaham. *The Complete Idiot's Guide to Shamanism*. Indianapolis: Alpha Books, 2002.

2. Orion, Loretta. *Never Again the Burning Times: Paganism Revived*, p. 142. Prospect Heights, IL: Waveland Press, 1995.

3. Goeller, Karen. "Common Yearnings: What Witchcraft and Shamanism Share," Chas Clifton, ed. *Witchcraft Today, Book Three: Witchcraft & Shamanism*, p. 61. St. Paul: Llewellyn Publications, 1994.

4. Clifton, Chas. "What Happened to Western Shamanism?" Chas Clifton, ed. *Witchcraft Today, Book Three: Witchcraft & Shamanism*, p. 85. St. Paul: Llewellyn Publications, 1994.

5. Harner, Michael. *The Way of the Shaman*, p. 25–6. New York: Bantam Books, 1982.

6. Walsh, Roger, M.D., Ph.D. *The Spirit of Shamanism*, p. 8. New York: G. P. Putnam's Sons, 1990.

7. Harner, xii-xiv.

Chapter 4

1. Goodman, Felicitas. *Where the Spirits Ride the Wind: Trance Journeys and Other Ecstatic Experiences.* Bloomington: Indiana University Press, 1990.

2. LaSirena, Robin. "Aspecting in the Service of Deity," *Reclaiming Quarterly, www.reclaimingquarterly.org/86/ rq-86-aspectingdeity. html* (October 8, 2005).

   Goodman, Felicitas and Nana Nauwald. *Ecstatic Trance: New Ritual Body Postures, A Workbook.* Havelte, Holland: Binkey Kok Publications, 2003.

3. You can use the recipe for consecration oil found in the "Consecration of Your Magical Tools" ritual, or choose oils that are pleasing to your senses and have magical meaning to you. A good source for this kind of information is: Cunningham, Scott. *The Complete Book of Incense, Oils & Brews.* St. Paul: Lewellyn Publications, 1989.

BIBLIOGRAPHY

There are three books on shamanic journeywork that I recommend to beginning students:

Cowan, Tom. *Shamanism: As a Practice for Daily Life.* Berkeley: Crossing Press, 1996.

A lyrical, wise, and beautiful look at the Celtic influences on shamanic practice.

Harner, Michael. *The Way of the Shaman.* San Francisco: HarperSanFrancisco, 1990.

The classic work that brought Shamanism into the awareness of mainstream culture, and coined the term "core Shamanism." Harner and his associates now run The Foundation for Shamanic Studies, which has workshops around the world in introductory and advanced techniques in core Shamanism. You can also visit *www.Shamanism.org* for more information.

Ingerman, Sandra. *Shamanic Journeying: A Beginner's Guide.* Boulder, CO: Sounds True, 2004.

One of the most respected voices in NeoShamanism, Ingerman has written books on soul retrieval. This book contains a drumming CD. You can visit her website at *www.shamanicvisions.com.*

For more information on animal and nature spirits that appear in your meditations, consult natural history field guides such as Peterson Field Guides to understand their natural behavior. For more symbolic, esoteric, and magical sources, consult:

Andrews, Ted. *Animal Speak: The Spiritual & Magical Powers of Creatures Great & Small.* St. Paul, MN: Llewellyn Publications, 2002.

Andrews, Ted. *Animal Wise: The Spirit Language and Signs of Nature.* Jackson, TN: Dragonhawk Publishing, 1999.

Andrews, Ted. *Nature-Speak: Signs, Omens and Messages in Nature.* Jackson, TN: Dragonhawk Publishing, 2003.

Andrews' books combine a strong knowledge of natural behavior with esoteric and magical meanings.

Galenorn, Yasmine. *Totem Magic: Dance of the Shapeshifter.* Berkeley: Crossing Press, 2004.

A magical book on practical ways a modern day witch can work with totems and animal spirits in powerful, transforming ways.

Other books on Shamanism and shamanic journeywork:

Berggren, Karen. *Circle of Shaman: Healing Through Ecstasy, Rhythm, and Myth.* Rochester, VT: Destiny Books, 1998.

Dolfyn. *Shamanic Wisdom: Nature Spirituality, Sacred Power and Earth Ecstasy.* Oakland, CA: Earthspirit, Inc., 1990.

Drake, Ann. *Healing of the Soul: Shamanism & Psyche.* Ithaca, NY: BUSCA, Inc., 2004.

Ingerman, Sandra. *Soul Retrieval: Mending the Fragmented Self.* San Francisco: HarperSanFrancisco, 1991.

Penczak, Christopher. *The Temple of Shamanic Witchcraft: Shadows, Spirits, and the Healing Journey.* St. Paul, MN: Llewellyn Publications, 2005.

Sarangerel. *Chosen by the Spirits: Following Your Shamanic Calling.* Rochester, VT: Destiny Books, 2001.

Tedlock, Barbara. *The Woman in the Shaman's Body: Reclaiming the Feminine in Religion and Medicine.* New York: Bantam Books, 2005.

Books on Wicca and Witchcraft:

Adler, Margot. *Drawing Down the Moon: Witches, Druids, Goddess-Worshippers, and Other Pagans in America Today.* New York: Penguin Group, 1986.

Campanelli, Pauline. *Ancient Ways: Reclaiming Pagan Traditions.* St. Paul, MN: Llewellyn Publications, 1991.

Campanelli, Pauline. *Wheel of the Year: Living the Magical Life.* St. Paul, MN: Llewellyn Publications, 2000.

Coyle, T. Thorn. *Evolutionary Witchcraft.* New York: Jeremy P. Tarcher, 2004.

Cunningham, Scott. *Wicca: A Guide for the Solitary Practitioner.* St. Paul, MN: Llewellyn Publications, 2003.

Cunningham, Scott. *Living Wicca: A Further Guide for the Solitary Practitioner.* St. Paul, MN: Llewellyn Publications, 2003.

Curott, Phyllis. *Witchcrafting: A Spiritual Guide to Making Magic.* New York: Broadway Books, 2001.

Farrar, Janet and Stewart. *The Witches' God.* Blaine, WA: Phoenix Publishing, 1989.

Farrar, Janet and Stewart. *The Witches' Goddess.* Blaine, WA: Phoenix Publishing, 1987.

Green, Marian. *A Witch Alone: Thirteen Moons to Master Natural Magic.* London: Aquarian Press, 1991.

Hutton, Ronald. *The Triumph of the Moon: A History of Modern Pagan Witchcraft.* Oxford: Oxford University Press, 1999.

Starhawk. *The Spiral Dance: A Rebirth of the Ancient Religion of the Great Goddess.* San Francisco: HarperSanFrancisco, 1999.

Wood, Gail. *Rituals of the Dark Moon:13 Lunar Rites for a Magical Path.* St. Paul, MN: Llewellyn, 2001.